SAS/GRAPH® Software:
Introduction

Version 6
First Edition

SAS Institute Inc.
SAS Campus Drive
Cary, NC 27513

The correct bibliographic citation for this manual is as follows: SAS Institute Inc., *SAS/GRAPH® Software: Introduction, Version 6, First Edition*, Cary, NC: SAS Institute Inc., 1990. 122 pp.

SAS/GRAPH® Software: Introduction, Version 6, First Edition

Contents

Reference Aids

Figures

Special Topics

Credits

Documentation

Composition	Cynthia M. Hopkins, Blanche W. Phillips, Pamela A. Troutman, David S. Tyree
Gallery of Graphs Graphics	Marketing Division
Graphic Design	Creative Services Department
Proofreading	Gwen T. Colvin, Beth A. Heiney, Hanna P. Hicks, Toni P. Sherrill, Anna B. Williams
Technical Review	Shearin Bizzell, Donna Bravo, Cathy Brinsfield, Jack Bulkley, Roger Chenoweth, Betsy Corning, Sarah Darden, Gretel Easter, Anthony Friebel, Sean Gargan, John H. Gough IV, Craig Hales, Edie Jeffreys, Mike Kalt, Paul Karlok, Lelia McConnell, Himesh Patel, Julie M. Platt, Randy Poindexter, Bill Powers, Duane E. Ressler
Writing and Editing	Mark E. Britt, Shirley N. Garrett, Susan H. McCoy, Julie M. Platt, Philip R. Shelton, Helen Weeks

Software

Product development includes design, programming, debugging, support, and preliminary documentation. In the following list, developers who currently support the procedure or feature are indicated with an asterisk. Others provided specific assistance for this release or previous releases.

GANNO	Anthony Friebel*
GCHART	Jack Bulkley*, James H. Goodnight
GCONTOUR	Anthony Friebel, James H. Goodnight, Dave Jeffreys*, Jim Lee, Jade Walker
GDEVICE	Jade Walker*
GFONT	Anthony Friebel*, Dale D. Ingold, Jim Lee, Doug Walker
GKEYMAP	Anthony Friebel*, Doug Walker
GMAP	James H. Goodnight, Jim Lee*
GOPTIONS	Sheila Fitzgerald Evans*, Dale D. Ingold, Doug Walker
GPLOT	David M. DeLong, Anthony Friebel, James H. Goodnight, Nitin Patel*, Jane Pierce
GPRINT	Jack Bulkley*, James H. Goodnight
GPROJECT	Dale D. Ingold, Dave Jeffreys*, Jade Walker

GREDUCE	David M. DeLong, Dave Jeffreys*
GREMOVE	Jack Bulkley, James H. Goodnight, Dave Jeffreys*
GREPLAY	Rick Edwards, Mark Mendenhall*, Stuart Nisbet
GSLIDE	Dale D. Ingold, Jade Walker*
GTESTIT	Craige Hales, Jade Walker*
G3D	Craige Hales, Jim Lee, Stuart Nisbet*, Nitin Patel, Jade Walker
G3GRID	David M. DeLong, Jane Pierce*
Fonts	Anthony Friebel*, Jim Lee, Doug Walker
Maps	Jack Bulkley, Dave Jeffreys*
Device Drivers	Jack Bulkley, Robert J. Dolan, Anthony Friebel, Howard Houston*, Mike Kalt, Jack S. Lin, Woody Middleton, Nitin Patel, Jade Walker, Jim Ward
Annotate Facility	Anthony Friebel*
Global Statements	Jack Bulkley, Sheila Fitzgerald Evans*, Anthony Friebel, Dale D. Ingold, Doug Walker
GSUBLIB	Valerie Blettner, Jack Bulkley, Rick Edwards, Anthony Friebel, Howard Houston, Jim Lee*, Doug Walker, Jade Walker
GWINDOW	Art Barnes*, Rick Edwards, Phil Herold, Howard Houston, Jim Lee, Woody Middleton, Jim Weathers
DATA Step Graphics Interface	Jade Walker*
Statement Windows	Sheila Fitzgerald Evans*
Samples and Testing	Jim Beamon, Donna Bravo*, Betsy Corning, Ottis R. Cowper, Sheila Fitzgerald Evans, John H. Gough IV, Marilyn M. Hanson, Barry F. Hicks, Julie McAlpine Platt, Duane E. Ressler

Support Groups

Technical Support	Donna M. Aikman, Michael R. Baker, Gretel Easter, Mike Kalt, Sheri J. King, Richard D. Lee, Michael R. Long, Liza Lucas, Lelia M. McConnell, Martin L. Mincey, Randall D. Poindexter, Jude L. Redman, Peter H. Ruzsa, Linda J. Spanton
Quality Assurance Testing	Brendan R. Bailey, Shearin Bizzell, Roger Chenoweth, Brad L. Chisholm, Sarah Darden, Libby Gell, Edie Jeffreys, Paul J. Karlok, Ria Murakeozy, Himesh G. Patel

Using This Book

Purpose

SAS/GRAPH Software: Introduction, Version 6, First Edition provides basic introductory material about SAS/GRAPH software, Release 6.06, and demonstrates how to produce simple charts, maps, plots, and text slides.

Read the remainder of "Using This Book" to learn the prerequisites you should have to use this book, how you can be most effective in using it, and the conventions that are used in text and sample SAS programs.

When you finish using this book, please complete the Your Turn page provided at the end of this book. We want to know what you think about *SAS/GRAPH Software: Introduction*, and your response to the questions on the Your Turn page helps us to improve the book.

Audience

SAS/GRAPH Software: Introduction is intended for those of you who want or need to learn how to use SAS/GRAPH software and who consider yourselves new users, whether you are computer-naive or computer-literate.

Prerequisites

Before being able to use *SAS/GRAPH Software: Introduction* effectively, you should have

☐ become familiar with base SAS software to the extent revealed in the *SAS Introductory Guide, Third Edition*

☐ access to a graphics terminal.

How to Use This Book

This section provides an overview of the information in and organization of this book.

Organization

This book is divided into eight chapters that take you step-by-step through commonly used features of SAS/GRAPH software. Each chapter builds on the previous one; you should work through them in order.

Chapter 1, "Producing Graphics Output in the SAS System"
shows how you can set up your monitor to display the graphics you create. In addition, it introduces options you can use to print and store graphics.

Chapter 2, "Titles and Footnotes"
shows you how to produce titles and footnotes for graphics. This topic is presented early in the book because titles and footnotes are handled independently of graphs and work the same way for all the types of graphs you produce.

Chapter 3, "Bar Charts"
shows you how to present statistical information in the form of vertical and horizontal bar charts, which are useful in emphasizing exact magnitudes and differences. It also gives you a brief introduction to block charts, which are useful in emphasizing relative magnitudes and differences.

Chapter 4, "Pie Charts"
shows you how to present statistical information in the form of a pie chart, which is useful in showing how a part of the data relates to the whole. It also gives you a brief introduction to star charts, which are useful in showing if an activity is in balance with its counterparts or is under control.

Chapter 5, "Plots"
shows you how to present statistical information in the form of two-dimensional plots, which are an effective way to show a trend in data over a period of time, or to show the relationship of one variable to another.

Chapter 6, "Maps"
shows you how to present statistical information in the form of maps. Using maps, you can summarize data that vary according to geographic area, highlight regional differences, and show trends and variations of data between geographic areas.

Chapter 7, "Text Slides"
shows you how to create presentation text slides using titles, footnotes, and notes.

Chapter 8, "Gallery of Graphs"
displays other graphs you can produce using SAS/GRAPH software and related SAS software. They are beyond the scope of this book to cover more fully.

What You Should Read

In order to gain full benefit from *SAS/GRAPH Software: Introduction*, you should read every chapter, starting with the first. Each chapter of this book builds on what you have learned in the previous chapters, so if you skip early chapters you may not be prepared for the material in later chapters.

Reference Aids

SAS/GRAPH Software: Introduction has been organized with the understanding that you will read it from cover to cover. However, after you have gone through this book the first time you may want to refer to it again. The following sections will help you locate the information you need:

Contents
: lists the chapters with their page numbers. Each chapter includes a table of contents that lists the sections of that chapter and their page numbers.

Reference Aids
: lists page numbers for all displays and figures in the book.

Glossary
: provides definitions of SAS/GRAPH terms and general SAS terms you find in the chapters.

Index
: provides the page numbers where specific topics, procedures, statements, and options are discussed.

Conventions

This section explains the various conventions used in presenting text, examples, and output.

Typographical Conventions

You will see several type styles and an alternate text color used in this book. The following list explains the meaning of each style and the color:

roman
: is the standard type style used for most text in this book.

UPPERCASE ROMAN
: is used for SAS statements, variable names, and other SAS language elements when they appear in the text. However, you can enter these elements in your own SAS programs in lowercase, uppercase, or a mixture of the two.

italic
: is used for generic terms that represent values you must supply. This style is also used for special terms defined in the text.

<dl>
<dt><code>monospace</code></dt>
<dd>is used for examples of SAS programs and commands. This style is also used for character values when they appear in text.</dd>

<dt><code>red monospace</code></dt>
<dd>is used for portions of sample SAS programs that have changed from the previous SAS programs you have entered.</dd>
</dl>

Conventions for Examples and Output

Each of the chapters includes examples you will work through, illustrating some of the features of SAS/GRAPH software. The examples in this book were designed to be displayed on a graphics monitor rather than a printer or plotter. Each example contains

- an explanation of the nature of the example
- the sample SAS program for you to submit
- a sample of the output you should see on your monitor
- an explanation of the results.

The dimensions of the graphics output area vary across devices and when using SAS/GRAPH windows, if available. The dimensions may affect aspects of the graphics output (for example, the appearance of axes and the spacing of tick marks).

For educational purposes, this book instructs you to choose a variety of colors, patterns, and type styles to show you the range of options SAS/GRAPH software gives you. Take into consideration that the effect of this variety is to produce some graphs that do not look as polished as they would with fewer options; you should always follow good design standards when creating your graphs.

Some of the examples rely on the default colors of the device to draw a graph. The default colors of devices vary and may cause your graph to use colors different from the colors presented in the book.

The examples in this book do not specify actual names for the file structures used for SAS data libraries or for external files. This is because different operating systems and different computing installations use different conventions for naming files and directories. Instead, the examples refer to storage locations generically. For example, a FILENAME statement to assign the fileref MYFILE would be shown as

```
filename myfile 'external-file';
```

For *external-file* you should supply a fully qualified filename, using the form required for your operating system. If you are unsure of the requirements at your site, see your SAS Software Consultant for more information, or refer to the documentation for using the SAS System under the operating system for the hardware at your site.

Using the SAS System

SAS/GRAPH software is part of the SAS System, a strategic application system for all phases of data access, data management, data analysis, and presentation. The inside front cover shows how SAS system products fit into various application categories.

SAS Applications Are Portable

SAS software runs on many host systems: personal computers, workstations, minicomputers, and mainframes. Applications developed on one host run compatibly on any of the other hosts; SAS applications and programs are fully portable.

Different Ways to Use the SAS System

There are two different ways to use the SAS System. One way is to use SAS programs; the other is to use SAS/ASSIST software, an easy, menu-driven interface to SAS features. This book tutors you in using SAS/GRAPH programs.

User Interfaces for the SAS System

The SAS System

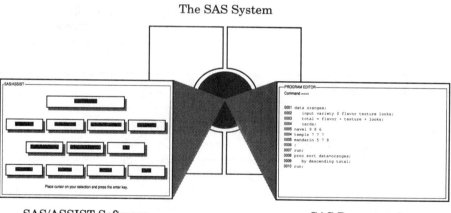

SAS/ASSIST Software   SAS Programming

SAS/ASSIST software is recommended for general users. General users and applications programmers may also want to use the simple SAS programming language to develop specialized programs and applications. The SAS System also provides a fourth-generation applications development environment, which can be used to build customized information systems quickly and easily.

Running Programs in This Book

When you are using SAS programs, you have a choice of several *execution modes,* that is, methods of running SAS programs and displaying output.

Execution Modes for Programs

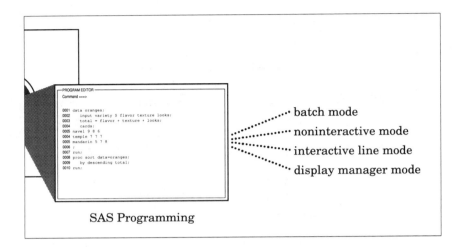

SAS Programming

Throughout most of this book none of the modes listed above is singled out; however, in a few places, using the SAS Display Manager System, because of its windowing capabilities, is the easiest and most effective mode available. In these cases, the functionalities of the software are described mainly for display manager, with Special Topic boxes enclosing directions for other available methods.

About the Colors in This Book

If the program does not explicitly specify colors for elements such as titles and patterns, SAS/GRAPH automatically selects colors from the output device's colors list. Because different devices support different sets of colors, the colors used by the program may vary from one device to another. As a result, the colors displayed on your output device may be different from those shown in this book.

Information You Need

This section outlines information you should know before you attempt to run the examples in this book. Record this information in the table at the bottom of this page.

Support Personnel

Record the name of the SAS Software Consultant and system administrator at your site in the space provided. Also record the names of anyone else you regularly turn to for help with running SAS/GRAPH software.

Sample Library

The source code for examples that produce output is provided in the SAS Sample Library. The sample library is provided to each site along with the SAS System. Ask your SAS Software Consultant for the location of the SAS Sample Library at your site.

SAS Software Consultant: _____ Phone: _____

SAS Software Representative: _____ Phone: _____

System Administrator: _____ Phone: _____

Other System Personnel: _____ Phone: _____

_____ Phone: _____

_____ Phone: _____

_____ Phone: _____

SAS Sample Library Location: _____

SAS/GRAPH Map Data Sets Location: _____

Additional Notes:

Additional Documentation

SAS Institute provides many publications about products of the SAS System and how to use them on specific hosts. For a complete list of SAS publications, you should refer to the current *Publications Catalog*. The catalog is produced twice a year. You can order a free copy of the catalog by writing to

> SAS Institute Inc.
> SAS Campus Drive
> Cary, NC 27513
> 919-677-8000

The following sections list books that provide more information about SAS/GRAPH software and related topics.

Documentation for SAS/GRAPH Software

In addition to *SAS/GRAPH Software: Introduction*, you will find these other documents helpful when using SAS/GRAPH software:

☐ *SAS/GRAPH Software: Examples, Version 6, First Edition* (order #A56022) provides examples of presentation-quality graphs.

☐ *SAS/GRAPH Software: Reference, Version 6, First Edition, Volume 1* and *Volume 2* (order #A56020) provide detailed reference information about SAS/GRAPH software.

☐ *SAS/GRAPH Software: Syntax, Version 6, First Edition* (order #A56024) provides quick reference to the syntax for SAS/GRAPH software.

☐ *SAS/GRAPH Software: Usage, Version 6, First Edition* (order #A56021) provides task-oriented examples of the major features of SAS/GRAPH software.

☐ *SAS/GRAPH Software: Using Graphics Devices* for your host environment provides information about SAS/GRAPH device drivers, metagraphics drivers, and operating-specific information about graphics options and device parameters.

☐ SAS companion or other SAS documentation for your host environment provides information about the host-specific features of the SAS System in your environment.

Documentation for Other SAS Software

This section lists other books you may need or may find helpful when using SAS/GRAPH software.

☐ *SAS Introductory Guide, Third Edition* (order #A5685) gets you started if you are unfamiliar with the SAS System or any other programming language.

□ *SAS Language: Reference, Version 6, First Edition* (order #A56076) provides detailed reference information about SAS language statements, functions, formats, and informats; the SAS Display Manager System; the SAS Text Editor; or any other element of base SAS software except for procedures.

□ *SAS Procedures Guide, Version 6, Third Edition* (order #A56080) provides detailed reference information about the procedures in base SAS software.

□ *SAS Language and Procedures: Usage, Version 6, First Edition* (order #A56075) provides task-oriented examples of the major features of base SAS software.

Chapter 1 Producing Graphics Output in the SAS System

Introduction

When you use SAS/GRAPH software, you run programs to produce graphics. Once they are created, you can

☐ display graphics on your monitor

☐ print graphics on a printer, slide camera, or plotter

☐ store graphics, either in a host file or SAS catalog.

This chapter shows how you can set up your monitor to display the graphics you create.

Displaying a List of Device Drivers for Your Monitor

To display the graphs you will create in this book on your monitor, you must first select a SAS/GRAPH device driver to match the monitor you use to view graphics. To select a device driver, take the following steps:

1. Begin a new SAS session.

2. If you are using the SAS Display Manager System, invoke the GDEVICE procedure by entering the following program, then pressing the SUBMIT key (or entering SUBMIT on the command line). If you are not using display manager, see the Special Topic box on the next page. Submit the following program statements to display a list of device drivers:

```
proc gdevice;
run;
```

A partial list of the device drivers is shown in Output 1.1.

Output 1.1
Displaying a List
of Device Drivers

```
    Name      Type    Description                            Updated

_   AGS1000   DEV     AGS 1000 terminal                      01/08/90
_   APLPLUS   DEV     Apple Laserwriter Plus (PostScript)    01/08/90
_   APPLELW   DEV     Apple Laserwriter (PostScript)         01/08/90
_   CAL81     DEV     CalComp 81 plotter                     01/08/90
_   CAL84     DEV     CalComp 84 plotter                     01/08/90
_   CGM       DEV     CGM generator--binary output           01/08/90
_   CGMC      DEV     CGM generator w/colors--binary output  01/08/90
_   CGMCHAR   DEV     CGM generator--character format        01/08/90
_   CGMCLEAR  DEV     CGM generator--Clear text format       01/08/90
_   CGMCRT    DEV     CGM for CRTs--binary format            01/08/90
_   CGMCRTCH  DEV     CGM for CRTs--character format         01/08/90
_   CGMCRTCL  DEV     CGM for CRTs--clear text format        01/08/90
_   CGMFL     DEV     CGM binary for Lotus Freelance rel 3.0 01/08/90
_   CGMFLM    DEV     CGM binary monochrome - Lotus Freelance 01/08/90
_   CGMGG     DEV     CGM driver for H-P Graphics Gallery 3.0 01/08/90
_   CGMHG     DEV     CGM color for Harvard Graphics 2.12    01/08/90
_   CGMHGM    DEV     CGM mono for Harvard Graphics 2.12     01/08/90
_   CGMIMG    DEV     CGM color for Image Builder            01/08/90
_   CGMPIX    DEV     CGM driver for Pixie and Mirage        01/08/90
_   CGMVP     DEV     CGM binary format for Ventura Publishing 01/08/90
_   CGMWP     DEV     CGM binary format for Word Perfect rel 5 01/08/90
_   CGMWPL    DEV     CGM for Word Perfect rel 5 Landscape   01/08/90
_   CGRAFIX   DEV     QMS Colorgrafix printer                01/08/90
_   CGRAFIXA  DEV     QMS Colorgrafix printer--A size paper  01/08/90
_   CHARDRV   DEV     Generic Character driver--80 columns   01/08/90
_   CHARDRVW  DEV     Generic Character driver--132 columns  01/08/90
```

Special Topic: Invoking the GDEVICE Procedure in Line Mode

If you are not using display manager, list the available device drivers by submitting the following program statements:

```
proc gdevice nofs;
    list _all_;
run;
```

The device driver list appears in the SAS log.

Selecting a Device Driver for Your Monitor

Scan the displayed list of available device drivers, which looks similar to Output 1.1, and write down the name of the device driver (listed in the Name column) that matches the description of your terminal (listed in the Description column). You may need to use the FIND command.

End the GDEVICE procedure, then set the device driver in your SAS session by submitting the following GOPTIONS statement. Replace *device-driver-name* with the device driver name you found in the list in Output 1.1.

```
goptions device=device-driver-name;
```

Graphics options (GOPTIONS) stay in effect for the duration of your SAS session, so the SAS System uses the device driver you specified until you

□ end your SAS session

□ specify another output device

□ use the GOPTIONS RESET= option.

Controlling the Display of Graphics Output

A major feature of SAS/GRAPH software is that it automatically uses default colors, type fonts, and fill patterns, allowing you to create graphs with a minimum number of statements. You can change many of these defaults with the GOPTIONS statement. You can use this statement to

□ control your output device

□ control the way graphics are displayed.

There are many options you can specify to control your graphics. To see the choices you have, submit the following program statements:

```
proc goptions;
run;
```

A partial list of available options is shown in Output 1.2.

Output 1.2
*Viewing the
Current Settings of
Graphics Options*

```
fcache=3                      Number of software fonts to keep in memory
fill                          Use hardware rectangle fill generator
fillinc=                      Fill increment to use on software polygon
                              fills.
ftext=                        Default text font
ftitle=                       Default font for first title
gaccess=''                    Output format for graphics stream
gclass=G                      IBM3287 sysout class
gcopies=(0, 20)               Number of output copies
gddmcopy=FSCOPY               GDDM driver hardcopy type
gddmnickname=                 GDDM nickname
gddmtoken=                    GDDM token
gdest=LOCAL                   IBM3287 sysout destination
gend=                         Buffer termination string
gepilog=                      Device termination string
gforms=                       IBM3287 sysout forms code
nogopt10                      Miscellaneous
nogopt11                      Miscellaneous
nogopt12                      Miscellaneous
nogopt13                      Miscellaneous
nogopt14                      Miscellaneous
nogopt15                      Miscellaneous
goutmode=APPEND               GOUT catalog mode: APPEND or REPLACE
gouttype=INDEPENDENT          Graphics segment type
gprolog=                      Device initialization string
gprotocol=                    Graphics protocol converter driver name
gsflen=                       Length of Graphics Stream File records
gsfmode=PORT                  Graphics Stream File access mode
```

The GOPTIONS procedure displays a log listing all the graphics options you can set or change using the GOPTIONS statement.

Scroll through the log listing. In general, you need to set only a few options to produce a given graph; if you don't set any, SAS/GRAPH software uses its internal defaults for the options to produce the graph.

Setting Graphics Options for This Book's Examples

For the instructional purposes of this book, there are a few graphics options you need to use. Submit the following program statement to set six options:

```
goptions gunit=pct
         cback=white
         htitle=6
         htext=3
         ftext=swissb
         ctext=blue;
```

□ The GUNIT= option sets the units of character height measurement to percentage of display height.

□ The CBACK= option sets the background color of your monitor to white.

□ The HTITLE= option sets the text height for the first title to 6 (in units of percent of the display height).

□ The HTEXT= option sets the text height for all text on graphs to 3 (in units of percent of the display height).

□ The FTEXT= option sets the text font to SWISSB for all text on graphs.

□ The CTEXT= option sets the text color to BLUE for all text on graphs.

By setting your options as shown above, you ensure that the graphs appearing on your display look as much as possible like the examples in this book.

Identifying the Source of Sample Data

For the examples in this book you will be using data from three files of the sample library supplied by SAS Institute. Take the following steps to access this sample data.

Note: For more information about using sample data, see "Conventions for Examples and Output" in "Using This Book." To find the location of your sample library, see your SAS Software Consultant.

1. Access the sample data by defining a *fileref*. To define a fileref, submit the following FILENAME statement each time you begin a new SAS session:

```
filename data 'sample-library-location';
```

2. Now you can access the files in this library by submitting a %INCLUDE statement to create each of three SAS data sets. The filenames for the three files you need for this book are listed below.

   □ GI01N01 is used in Chapter 5, "Plots."

   □ GI01N02 is used in Chapter 6, "Maps."

   □ GI01N03 is used in Chapter 3, "Bar Charts," and Chapter 4, "Pie Charts."

   Note: Depending on your operating system and the naming conventions at your site, the filenames in your sample library may be slightly different (for example, the file GI01N01 may appear as GI01N01.SAS).

3. Submit the following statement to include each SAS data set you will need. For example, if you need just one of the SAS data sets for a specific chapter in this book, submit a %INCLUDE statement for that data set only, but if you plan to go through all chapters, submit a %INCLUDE statement for each data set.

```
%include data (filename);
```

Chapter **2** Titles and Footnotes

Introduction

This chapter shows you how to produce titles and footnotes for graphics. The topic is presented early in this book because titles and footnotes are handled independently of graphs and work the same way for all of the types of graphs you produce.

Titles and footnotes are used to convey additional information about your graph or to add emphasis. You include titles and footnotes in your graphs by using TITLE and FOOTNOTE statements. This chapter shows you how to use them to

□   produce multiple titles and footnotes

□   change and delete TITLE and FOOTNOTE definitions

□   control height and font.

Global options remain in effect throughout a SAS session. Before you begin this chapter, make sure that no global options are still in effect by submitting the following statement:

```
goptions reset=global;
```

Note: If you have not already done so in your current SAS session, enter the following GOPTIONS statement to make sure your output looks as much as possible like the examples in this book.

```
goptions gunit=pct
        cback=white
        htitle=6
        htext=3
        ftext=swissb
        ctext=blue;
```

Writing Titles and Footnotes

TITLE and FOOTNOTE statements can appear anywhere in your SAS program, and once they are defined, the titles and footnotes remain in effect until they are canceled or the SAS session is ended. The GSLIDE procedure can be used to show titles and footnotes in a graph.

Submit the following SAS program to create a text display, or slide, that uses one title and one footnote:

```
title1 'Eastern Widgets Inc.';
footnote1 'Bar, Pie, and Block Charts';

proc gslide;
run;
```

The results are shown in Output 2.1.

▶ *Caution* . . . . *If you omit either the opening or closing quotation mark in a title or footnote statement, an error message will be displayed in the log.*
To correct the error in the SAS program, add the missing quotation mark to the appropriate statement, insert a single quotation mark followed by a semicolon (';) at the beginning of the SAS program, and resubmit it. ▲

Output 2.1
Generating Titles
and Footnotes

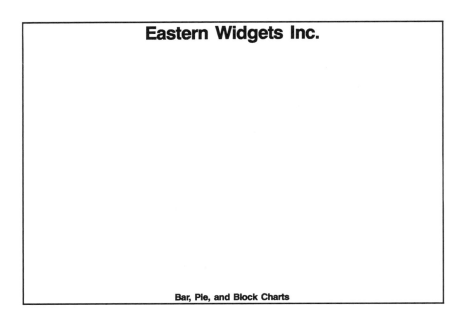

This example illustrates the following features:

□ The PROC GSLIDE statement runs the GSLIDE procedure to create the slide.

□ The TITLE1 statement defines the text to be used as the main title and places it on line 1 of the slide. By default, titles are centered on their respective lines.

- □ The font used comes from the FTEXT= graphics option you submitted earlier.

- □ The height for the first title comes from the HTITLE= graphics option. The height for the footnote comes from the HTEXT= graphics option.

- □ The FOOTNOTE1 statement defines the text to be used in the footnote at the bottom of the slide. By default, the footnote is centered on the line.

Using Multiple Titles and Footnotes

On slides or graphs, you can use up to ten titles and ten footnotes. If you want to add more information on the output you just created, you can define additional titles and footnotes.

Submit the following program statements to create multiple titles and footnotes:

```
title3 'Manufacturing and Sales Data';
title5 'Atlanta and Boston Sales Branches';
title7 'First Quarter, 1990';
footnote2 'Tracking Three Parts';

proc gslide;
run;
```

The results are shown in Output 2.2.

Output 2.2
Generating
Multiple Titles
and Footnotes

Eastern Widgets Inc.

Manufacturing and Sales Data

Atlanta and Boston Sales Branches

First Quarter, 1990

Bar, Pie, and Block Charts
Tracking Three Parts

This example illustrates the following features:

- □ The TITLE3 statement adds a second title and places it on line 3 of the slide. Likewise, the TITLE5 and TITLE7 statements place titles on lines 5 and 7 of the slide. Because you did not use a TITLE2, TITLE4, or TITLE6 statement, lines 2, 4, and 6 are blank.

- □ The FOOTNOTE2 statement places a second footnote on the slide.

- □ The first title and footnote are displayed even though you did not specify them again in your SAS statements. Titles and footnotes are global: once defined, they are printed on all graphic displays until you cancel or change a specific TITLE or FOOTNOTE definition or a lower-numbered title or footnote, or until you end the SAS session.

Changing Titles and Footnotes

To change a title (or footnote) that has already been defined, issue another TITLE statement that has the same number as the title you want to change. For example, to change the title on line 5, submit the following program statements:

```
title5 'Sales Branches: Atlanta and Boston';

proc gslide;
run;
```

The results are shown in Output 2.3.

Output 2.3
Changing Titles
and Footnotes

Eastern Widgets Inc.

Manufacturing and Sales Data

Sales Branches: Atlanta and Boston

Bar, Pie, and Block Charts
Tracking Three Parts

This example illustrates the following features:

□ The new TITLE5 statement defines a new title for line 5 and cancels the previous title on line 5.

□ The new TITLE5 statement also deletes the title on line 7. Changing a title cancels *all* titles that were previously printed below that title on the slide. The same is true for footnotes.

Deleting Titles and Footnotes

Deleting a title (or footnote) has the same effect as changing the title. You can delete a title by using a null TITLE statement.

Submit the following program statements to delete the title on line 3:

```
title3;

proc gslide;
run;
```

The results are shown in Output 2.4

Output 2.4
Deleting a Title

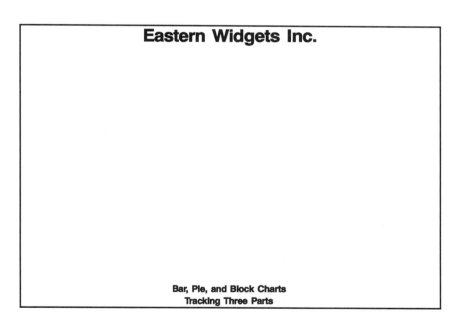

This example illustrates the following features:

□ The null TITLE statement cancels the title on line 3.

□ The title on line 5 is also deleted because a new TITLE statement cancels all titles that previously followed it.

Controlling Font and Height

In the previous examples, the font and the height of the characters were controlled by the FTEXT= and HTEXT= options that you used in the GOPTIONS statement in Chapter 1. However, by using certain options within TITLE and FOOTNOTE statements, you can override the effect of those options for your graphs.

Selecting a Font

There are a wide variety of fonts provided with SAS/GRAPH software. To display a list of available fonts, issue the following command:

```
catalog sashelp.fonts
```

After browsing through the list of fonts, display the character set for the DUPLEX font by submitting the following SAS program statements:

```
title1;
footnote1;

proc gfont name=duplex nobuild;
run;
```

The TITLE1 statement cancels all existing titles so they are not displayed on the GFONT output. The FOOTNOTE1 statement cancels all of the footnotes. The PROC GFONT statement identifies the DUPLEX font. The NOBUILD option displays the font's character set rather than indicating you want to create one.

Changing the Font

To use the DUPLEX font in your titles and footnotes, submit the following program statements:

```
title1 'Eastern Widgets Inc.';
title3 font=duplex 'Manufacturing and Sales Data';
title5 'Sales Branches: '
       font=duplex 'Atlanta and Boston';
title7 'First Quarter, 1990';
footnote1 'Bar, Pie, and Block Charts';
footnote2 'Tracking Three Parts';

proc gslide;
run;
```

The results are shown in Output 2.5.

Output 2.5
Changing the Text
Font

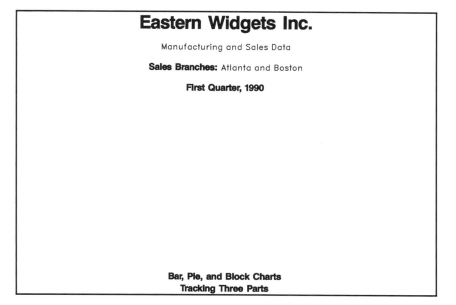

This example illustrates the following features:

□ The FONT= option assigns the DUPLEX font to the title on line 3 and part of the title on line 5.

□ The specified font remains in effect until another font is specified within the statement or until the statement ends.

□ For TITLE and FOOTNOTE statements that do not use the FONT= option, the GSLIDE procedure uses the default font, SWISSB, that you specified earlier in the GOPTIONS statement (in Chapter 1).

Changing the Height

Just as you can apply different fonts to your titles and footnotes, you can use different height specifications to control the size of characters in titles and footnotes. To change the height specifications, use the HEIGHT= option.

Submit the following program statements to change the heights of the titles on lines 3, 5, and 7 at the top of the slide, as well as the footnote on line 2 at the bottom of the slide:

```
title3 font=duplex
       height=5 pct 'Manufacturing and Sales Data';
title5 font=simplex
       height=4 pct 'Sales Branches: '
       font=triplex
       height=3 pct 'Atlanta and Boston';
title7 'First Quarter, 1990';
footnote2 height=.5 inch 'Tracking Three Parts';

proc gslide;
run;
```

The results are shown in Output 2.6.

Output 2.6
Changing the Text
Height

Eastern Widgets Inc.

Manufacturing and Sales Data

Sales Branches: Atlanta and Boston

First Quarter, 1990

Bar, Pie, and Block Charts
Tracking Three Parts

This example illustrates the following features:

□ The HEIGHT= option defines the height of the text for titles and footnotes. The specified height remains in effect until the height is changed within the statement or until the statement ends.

□ The TITLE3, TITLE5, and TITLE7 definitions specify the unit of height as percent (display percentage). For portability, use percents as the unit of height when you want the size of the characters to remain the same proportion to the size of the display device.

□ The FOOTNOTE2 definition specifies the unit of height as inches. Use inches and centimeters as the unit of height when you want the character size to remain the same regardless of the size of the display device.

□ The TITLE7 and FOOTNOTE1 definitions do not use the HEIGHT= option; therefore, the GSLIDE procedure uses the default height, 3 PCT, that you specified earlier with the GOPTIONS statement (in Chapter 1).

Special Topic: Good Text Design for Labels

Output 2.6 showed several different fonts on one slide to illustrate the use of options. For most graphs, you should pick one font and stick to it, varying size as needed. Using several fonts in one slide makes the slide less readable and less polished. Good type styles to use are

- **Century**
- **Swiss**
- **Zapf**

For more information about producing text slides, see Chapter 7, "Text Slides."

Chapter **3** Bar Charts

Introduction

In this chapter, you will learn to present statistical information in the form of a vertical or horizontal bar chart. Figure 3.1 shows a vertical and horizontal bar chart as well as a block chart, which you can also produce using the GCHART procedure.

Figure 3.1
Vertical Bar,
Horizontal Bar,
and Block Charts

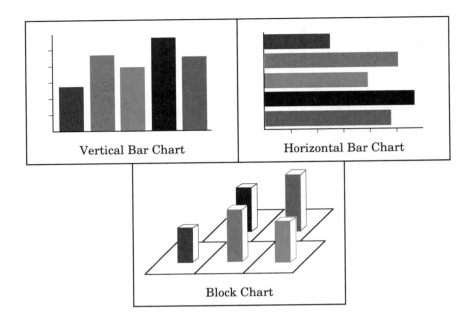

When deciding which type of chart you want to use, consider that

□ bar charts emphasize exact magnitudes and differences. Each vertical or horizontal bar represents the statistic for a value of a variable. The statistical values are shown on the response axis (vertical for vertical bar charts, horizontal for horizontal bar charts). Horizontal bar charts also display descriptive statistics to the right of each bar. For both charts, bars can be subdivided and grouped.

□ block charts emphasize relative magnitudes and differences three-dimensionally. Each vertical block represents the statistic for a value of a variable. Statistical values are displayed beneath the blocks. Like bars, blocks can be subdivided and grouped.

Whichever chart you choose, you use the same basic steps in the GCHART procedure with just a few variations for each chart.

Before beginning this chapter, make sure that no *global* options are still in effect by submitting the following program statement:

```
goptions reset=global;
```

Note: If you have not already done so in your current SAS session, enter the following GOPTIONS statement to make sure your output looks as much as possible like the examples in this book.

```
goptions gunit=pct
         cback=white
         htitle=6
         htext=3
         ftext=swissb
         ctext=blue;
```

Data for Sample Charts

In this chapter's examples, you will use a SAS data set called SALES (GI01N03 in the sample library provided), which contains sales information for three parts sold by a fictitious company during the first work week of 1990. For the examples in this chapter, you will use only five of the ten variables in the SAS data set.

BRANCH   is one of the two sales offices, either Atlanta or Boston.

PARTNUM   is a number assigned to the part.

DATE   is the date of sale.

AGENT   is the last name of the sales representative.

SALES   is the dollar amount of sales.

Note: If you did not create a SAS data set for these examples as shown in Chapter 1, "Producing Graphics Output in the SAS System," go back and do so now.

Understanding Chart Variables

When you use the GCHART procedure to create a vertical bar chart, you can chart values that are either *character variables* or *numeric variables*.
Character variable values can contain

□ letters (for example, `Poole`)

□ special characters (for example, #, @, and &)

□ numbers (for example, 59905)

□ any combination of letters, special characters, and numbers (for example, #59905P).

When you create a vertical bar chart for these character values, a separate bar is drawn for each value.
Numeric variable values contain just numbers. When you create a vertical bar chart for numeric variable values, each bar represents a range of values, such as 0 through 5. However, you can also chart numeric variables so that a separate bar is drawn for each value, such as 0, 1, 2, 3, 4, and 5.

Using GCHART Procedure Statistics

With the GCHART procedure you can produce charts based on six statistics.

frequency counts	total the number of observations for each charted value. This is the default statistic for PROC GCHART.
cumulative frequency counts	add the frequency count for the current charted value to the frequency counts of the preceding charted values.
percentages	divide the frequency of each charted value by the total frequency count for all charted values and multiplies the result by 100.
cumulative percentages	add the percentage for the current charted value to the percentage of the preceding charted values.
sum	totals the values for a specific variable for each charted value.
mean	averages the values for a specific variable for each charted value.

The GCHART procedure performs all of these calculations for you when you request them in PROC GCHART. You do not have to go through extra procedures (such as MEANS or SUMMARY procedures) to get the data into shape. For example, in your data set you can chart total sales, sales by date, sales by branch, or sales by branch by representative by part number without altering your data.

Creating Vertical Bar Charts

In this section you will learn how to create a vertical bar chart and make a few enhancements. For example, to show the number of transactions recorded by each agent (represented by values of the character variable AGENT) during the week using the data set SALES, submit the following three program statements:

```
proc gchart data=sales;
   vbar agent;
run;
```

The results are shown in Output 3.1.

Output 3.1
Creating a Simple
Vertical Bar Chart

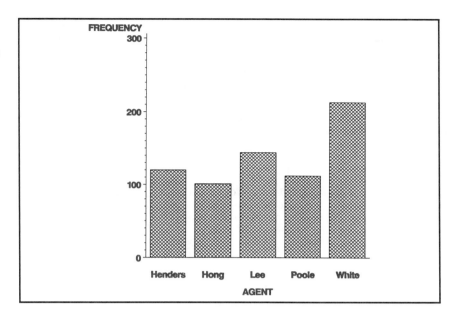

This example illustrates the following features:

□   The PROC GCHART statement specifies the procedure and data set.

□   The VBAR statement specifies the type of chart (vertical) and the variable (AGENT) to be charted.

□   The RUN statement begins the processing of statements.

□   The bars are arranged on the chart in ascending alphabetical order (of the variable values) starting from the left on the horizontal axis; the values are charted in ascending numerical order from the bottom up on the vertical axis.

Each *observation* in the data set you are using corresponds to a sale; Output 3.1 shows the total observations per sales agent. In other words, it shows how often each agent made a sale during the first work week of 1990, comparing the figures with one another. This example shows that during the week agent Henders made about 120 sales, Hong made about 100, Lee made about 150, and so on.

Charting Numeric Variables

This section shows you how to chart a numeric variable. In the following example, you will chart how often transactions of a certain dollar value take place.

To chart the company's number of sales transactions according to the amount of sale, remove the variable AGENT from the last program you entered, then add the variable SALES. In addition, to make your chart appear in a solid color, add the PATTERN statement, then submit the following program statements:

```
pattern1 value=solid;

proc gchart data=sales;
   vbar sales;
run;
```

The results are shown in Output 3.2.

Output 3.2
Charting a
Numeric Variable

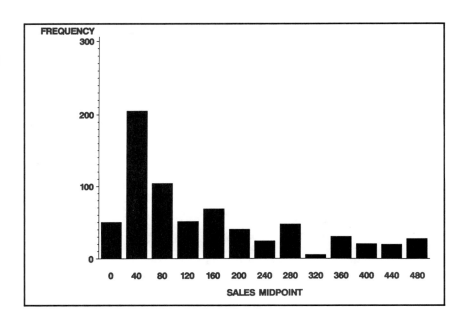

This example illustrates the following features:

□ The variable SALES is charted using the VBAR statement.

□ Each bar represents a range of numbers and is labeled with a number. This number is the middle of the range of numbers represented by that bar (except for the first bar, which is labeled with the lowest number represented). These numbers are called *midpoints*, which is why the horizontal axis is labeled SALES MIDPOINT.

□ The PATTERN statement uses the VALUE= option to fill the bars with a solid pattern, replacing the default pattern of crosshatched lines.

The bar labeled 0 represents the numbers below 20; the bar labeled 40 represents the numbers between 20 and 60. So, reading the chart you can see that the company made about 50 transactions for sales totaling less than 20 dollars, about 210 transactions for sales totaling between 20 and 60 dollars, and so on.

From a broader perspective, this chart shows that sales most frequently total between 20 and 100 dollars.

Charting Numeric Variable Values Individually

Sometimes you may want a separate bar for each distinct (or discrete) value of a numeric variable, such as when you create a chart for a date, year, part number, or ZIP code.

To show the frequency of sales on each of the five days recorded in the data set SALES, you need to make some changes in your program. In the VBAR statement, substitute the variable DATE for SALES and remove the semicolon. Then, add a slash and the DISCRETE option. Also, to display the variable DATE in a more readable form, instead of as a SAS date value (which show up as numbers), add the DATE7. format for the variable DATE.

Submit the following program statements:

```
pattern1 value=solid;

proc gchart data=sales;
    format date date7.;
    vbar date
        / discrete;
run;
```

The results are shown in Output 3.3.

Output 3.3
Charting Numeric
Variable Values
Individually

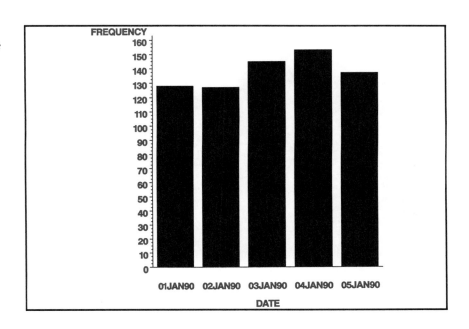

This example illustrates the following features:

□ The variable DATE is charted using the VBAR statement.

□ The DISCRETE option makes it possible for a separate bar to appear for each date value.

□ The DATE7. format converts the date underneath each bar from a SAS date value into a readable form. See *SAS Language: Reference, Version 6, First Edition* for additional date and time formats you can use.

The most sales occurred on the fourth day of the recording period; the fewest on the second day.

Grouping Bars

By using the GROUP= option, you can organize the bars of a vertical bar chart into groups based on a variable other than the one you are primarily charting.

To show the frequency of sales per day at each sales branch, add the GROUP= option and assign it the variable BRANCH. In addition, to override a previously set graphics option, enter a new GOPTIONS statement.

Submit the following program statements to group the vertical bars:

```
goptions htext=2;
pattern1 value=solid;

proc gchart data=sales;
   format date date7.;
   vbar date
        / discrete
            group=branch;
run;
```

The results are shown in Output 3.4.

Output 3.4
Grouping
Variables

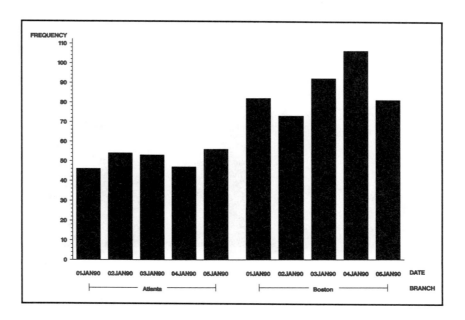

This example illustrates the following features:

□ The GROUP= option breaks the chart into two groups of bars. The first group of bars charts the results for the Atlanta branch; the second group charts the Boston branch. By comparing the bars, you can see that Boston had more sales transactions than Atlanta for the same week.

□ The GOPTIONS statement sets the text height to two percent of the display (overriding the previous setting of three percent) so the dates fit underneath the bars.

Subdividing Bars

In addition to grouping bars, you can subdivide, or stack, segments of each bar (based on the contribution of a variable) by using the SUBGROUP= option.

To show the frequency of sales per day according to part number, delete the GROUP= option and add the SUBGROUP= option, assigning it the variable PARTNUM. Also, change the text height back to its original setting using the GOPTIONS statement.

Submit the following program statements to subdivide the vertical bars:

```
goptions htext=3;
pattern1 value=solid;

proc gchart data=sales;
   format date date7.;
   vbar date
        / discrete
          subgroup=partnum;
run;
```

The results are shown in Output 3.5.

Output 3.5
Stacking Bars

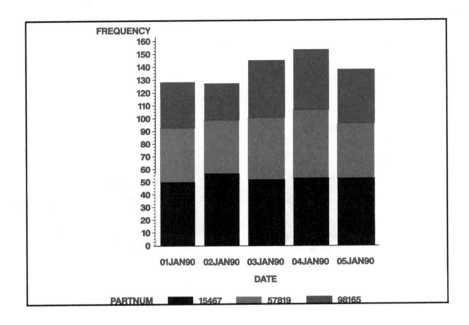

This example illustrates the following features:

□ The SUBGROUP= option stacks the three areas of each bar. Each area corresponds to a part number listed in the legend at the bottom of the chart, which automatically appears when the SUBGROUP= option is used. (The GROUP= option and the SUBGROUP= option can be used together.)

□ The GOPTIONS statement overrides the previous setting of the text height.

A quick glance shows you how often a part number sold relative to the other part numbers on any given day. For example, you can see that on 02JAN90, part number 98165 had fewer sales than the other two parts.

Specifying the Statistics Charted

The default statistic for the GCHART procedure is frequency of observations (how often a variable value is recorded). You can chart a different statistic by using the TYPE= option.

To show the cumulative frequency of sales per day according to part number, add the TYPE= option, assigning it the CFREQ statistic. Because the GOPTIONS statement is no longer needed, remove it.

Submit the following program statements to specify statistics for your chart:

```
pattern1 value=solid;

proc gchart data=sales;
   format date date7.;
   vbar date
        / discrete
          subgroup=partnum
          type=cfreq;
   run;
```

The results are shown in Output 3.6.

Output 3.6
Specifying a Statistic to Be Charted

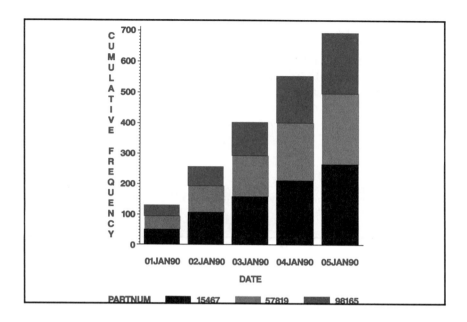

This example illustrates the following feature:

□   The TYPE= option, using the CFREQ statistic, shows that over the course of the week the number of overall sales were fairly balanced, as were sales for each part number. No one day added significantly more to the sales frequency total than any other day.

You can specify percentage and cumulative percentage of frequency in the same way you specified the cumulative frequency. However, if you want to display the total or average values of a variable, you must use the SUMVAR= option, which is illustrated in the next section.

Charting Summed Variables

To show the total daily sales value for each part number, change the TYPE= option to SUM and add the SUMVAR= option to total the variable SALES. In addition, because the results are shown in dollar amounts, use the DOLLAR7. format for the variable SALES.

Submit the following program statements to total the daily sales values for
each part number:

```
pattern1 value=solid;

proc gchart data=sales;
    format date date7. sales dollar7.;
    vbar date
        / discrete
          subgroup=partnum
          type=sum
          sumvar=sales;
run;
```

The results are shown in Output 3.7.

Output 3.7
Displaying the
Sum of Variables

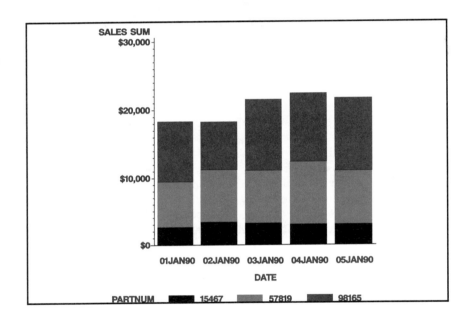

This example illustrates the following features:

□   The TYPE= option specifies the statistic, in this case SUM, for the
    SUMVAR= option. (SUM is the default statistic for the SUMVAR= option,
    so in this case it is not technically required. However, if you wanted to find
    the mean, you would have to enter TYPE=MEAN.)

□   The SUMVAR= option adds each day's values for the variable SALES,
    showing that the total sales value was highest on 04JAN90 and lowest on
    01JAN90 and 02JAN90.

□   The DOLLAR7. format caused the values on the vertical axis to appear with
    dollar signs and commas.

By looking at the subgroups, you can visually estimate how much of each
day's sales went to each part. For example, on 05JAN90, part number 98165
accounted for about 50% of the total sales value.

Enhancing a Bar Chart's Appearance

Now that you've learned how to create a bar chart, you need to learn how to add to and change its appearance. For example, you can

□ control the tick marks on the response axis

□ print statistics for each of a chart's bars

□ include titles, footnotes, and labels

□ change bar patterns and colors.

Changing the Response Axis

The GCHART procedure scales the response axis (vertical for vertical bar charts; horizontal for horizontal bar charts) and provides appropriate major tick marks by default. You can define a new axis with the AXIS statement, then include the AXIS definition in the VBAR statement with the RAXIS= option.

To change the response axis and tick marks so that the chart can be read more precisely, add an AXIS statement with the ORDER= option defining the tick marks to be 0 through 25000 by units of 5000. Then use the RAXIS= option to include the newly defined axis in the chart. In addition, because the TYPE=SUM option is not needed technically, delete it from the program.

Submit the following program statements to change the response axis:

```
axis1 order=(0 to 25000 by 5000);

pattern1 value=solid;

proc gchart data=sales;
   format date date7. sales dollar7.;
   vbar date
        / discrete
          subgroup=partnum
          sumvar=sales
          raxis=axis1;
run;
```

The results are shown in Output 3.8.

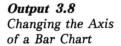

Output 3.8
Changing the Axis
of a Bar Chart

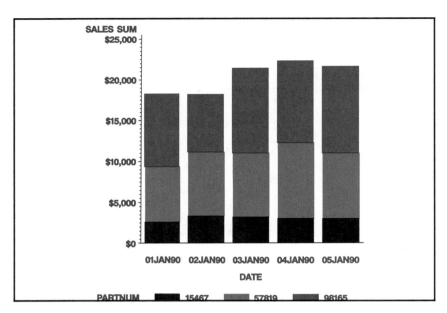

This example illustrates the following features:

□   The AXIS statement creates a new AXIS definition, with the ORDER=
option specifying the starting and ending tick marks, as well as the
increment of change.

□   The RAXIS= option includes the new AXIS definition in the chart.

□   Removing the TYPE= option does not affect the bar chart.

There are more numbers and tick marks on the response axis, making the
chart look more compact, but also easier to read exact values of the statistic.

Defining Axis Colors and Labels

You can use the AXIS statement to change the response axis in many different
ways; for instance, to change the color and add a label to the axis, include the
COLOR= and LABEL= options.

Submit the following program statements to change the definition of the axis:

```
axis1 order=(0 to 25000 by 5000)
     color=red
     label=('Sales Totals');

pattern1 value=solid;
```

```
proc gchart data=sales;
   format date date7. sales dollar7.;
   vbar date
        / discrete
          subgroup=partnum
          sumvar=sales
          raxis=axis1;
run;
```

The results are shown in Output 3.9.

Output 3.9
Changing the
Color and Label of
an Axis

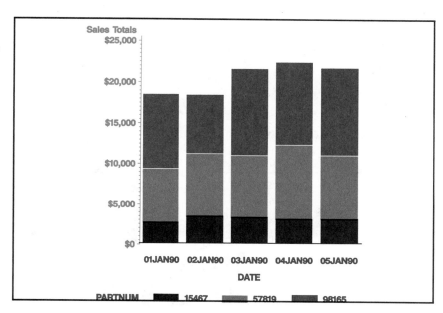

This example illustrates the following features:

□   The COLOR= option changes the color of the vertical axis to red.

□   The LABEL= option adds a label, Sales Totals, to the top of the axis.

Printing Statistics for Each Bar

You can print specific statistics at the top of each bar. For example, to show the sales totals for each day at the top of the bars, add the SUM option.

Submit the following program statements to print the SUM statistic above each bar:

```
axis1 order=(0 to 25000 by 5000)
      color=red
      label=('Sales Totals');

pattern1 value=solid;

proc gchart data=sales;
   format date date7. sales dollar7.;
   vbar date
        / discrete
          subgroup=partnum
          sumvar=sales
          raxis=axis1
          sum;
run;
```

The results are shown in Output 3.10.

Output 3.10
Printing Statistics
Above Each Bar

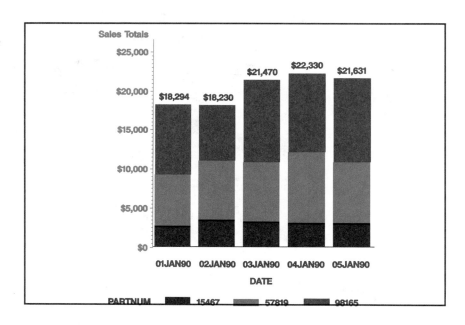

This example illustrates the following feature:

□ The SUM option displays the dollar amounts above each bar, showing the exact totals for each day's sales. For example, on 01JAN90 the sum of all sales was $18,294.

Note: You can request only one statistic per graph.

Including Titles, Footnotes, and Labels

You can add titles and footnotes to a vertical bar chart as you learned in Chapter 2, "Titles and Footnotes."

Submit the following program statements to add titles and a footnote to the previous example:

```
title1 height=5 pct 'Daily Sales Totals';
title2 font=simplex 'Subgrouped by Part Number';
footnote color=red font=simplex 'Data from WORK.SALES';
axis1 order=(0 to 25000 by 5000)
      color=red
      label=('Sales Totals');

pattern1 value=solid;

proc gchart data=sales;
   format date date7. sales dollar7.;
   vbar date
        / discrete
          subgroup=partnum
          sumvar=sales
          raxis=axis1
          sum;
run;
```

The results are shown in Output 3.11.

Output 3.11
Including Titles
and Footnotes

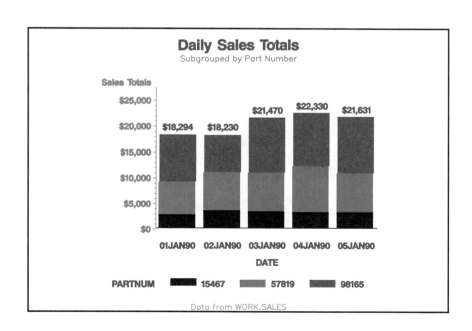

This example illustrates the following features:

□ The HEIGHT= option in the TITLE1 statement sets the height of the main title to five percent of the display. By default, titles and footnotes appear centered in relation to the chart.

□ The FONT= option in the TITLE2 and FOOTNOTE statements causes the title on line 2 and the footnote to be displayed in the SIMPLEX font.

□ The COLOR= option in the FOOTNOTE statement changes the footnote to red.

Adding Labels to Variables

You can add labels to variables by using the LABEL statement. After the PROC GCHART statement, add a LABEL statement assigning each charted variable a label.

Submit the following program statements to label your chart:

```
title1 height=5 pct 'Daily Sales Totals';
title2 font=simplex 'Subgrouped by Part Number';
footnote color=red font=simplex 'Data from WORK.SALES';
axis1 order=(0 to 25000 by 5000)
      color=red
      label=('Sales Totals');

pattern1 value=solid;

proc gchart data=sales;
   label sales='Total Sales'
         date='Date of Sale'
         partnum='Part Number';
   format date date7. sales dollar7.;
   vbar date
        / discrete
          subgroup=partnum
          sumvar=sales
          raxis=axis1
          sum;
run;
```

The results are shown in Output 3.12.

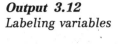

Output 3.12
Labeling variables

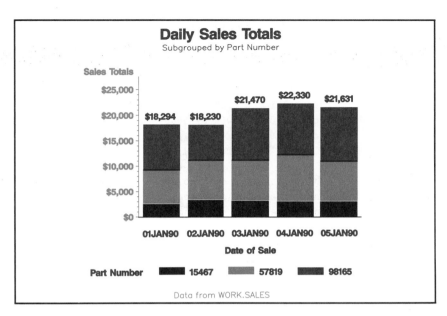

This example illustrates the following features:

□   The DATE= argument in the LABEL statement creates the label Date of Sale for the variable DATE.

□   The PARTNUM= argument creates the label Part Number for the variable PARTNUM.

□   The label for the variable SALES, however, is still Sales Totals (the label you gave it in the AXIS statement), not Total Sales, as you just labeled it. AXIS statement labels override LABEL statements.

Changing Bar Patterns and Colors

You can change the patterns and colors of the vertical bars by using the PATTERN statement to define pattern characteristics, then using the PATTERNID= option to determine when the pattern should change.

To change the patterns and colors of the subgroups, change one PATTERN statement and enter two others to define three pattern and color characteristics. Then enter the PATTERNID= option to change the patterns and colors for each subgroup. Also, because it is not being used, delete the label for the variable SALES that you entered in the last example.

Submit the following program statements to add patterns and colors to the vertical bars:

```
title1 height=5 pct 'Daily Sales Totals';
title2 font=simplex 'Subgrouped by Part Number';
footnote color=red font=simplex 'Data from WORK.SALES';
axis1 order=(0 to 25000 by 5000)
      color=red
      label=('Sales Totals');

pattern1 value=right color=blue;
pattern2 value=x3 color=green;
pattern3 value=solid color=red;

proc gchart data=sales;
   label date='Date of Sale'
         partnum='Part Number';
   format date date7. sales dollar7.;
   vbar date
       / discrete
         subgroup=partnum
         sumvar=sales
         raxis=axis1
         sum
         patternid=subgroup;
run;
```

The results are shown in Output 3.13.

Output 3.13
Changing Bar
Patterns and
Colors

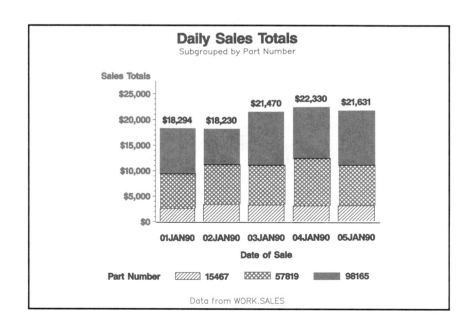

This example illustrates the following features:

□ In the PATTERN1 statement, the VALUE=RIGHT and COLOR=BLUE options fill the first subgroup (the bottom) with right-slanting blue lines.

□ In the PATTERN2 statement, the VALUE=X3 and COLOR=GREEN options fill the second subgroup (the middle) with crosshatched green lines using a shading density level of 3 (1 produces the lightest shading, 5 the heaviest).

□ In the PATTERN3 statement, the VALUE=SOLID and COLOR=RED options fill the third subgroup (the top) with the color red.

You now know how to create a basic vertical bar chart. There are many more options and statements not covered in this book that you can use to customize and improve the appearance of your chart. See Chapter 8, "Gallery of Graphs," and *SAS/GRAPH Software: Reference, Version 6, First Edition, Volume 1* and *Volume 2* for more information.

Creating and Enhancing Horizontal Bar Charts

You can create and enhance horizontal bar and block charts in much the same way you just produced vertical bar charts. For example, to chart the last vertical bar chart you produced as a horizontal bar chart, substitute the HBAR statement for the VBAR statement. Also, because statistics are displayed by default in horizontal bar charts, delete the SUM option. Finally, to make the chart look better, change all patterns to solid.

Submit the following program statements to create a horizontal bar chart:

```
title1 height=5 pct 'Daily Sales Totals';
title2 font=simplex 'Subgrouped by Part Number';
footnote color=red font=simplex 'Data from WORK.SALES';
axis1 order=(0 to 25000 by 5000)
      color=red
      label=('Sales Totals');

pattern1 value=solid color=blue;
pattern2 value=solid color=green;
pattern3 value=solid color=red;

proc gchart data=sales;
   label date='Date of Sale'
         partnum='Part Number';
   format date date7. sales dollar7.;
   hbar date
         / discrete
           subgroup=partnum
           sumvar=sales
           raxis=axis1
           patternid=subgroup;
run;
```

The results are shown in Output 3.14.

Output 3.14
Creating a
Horizontal Bar
Chart

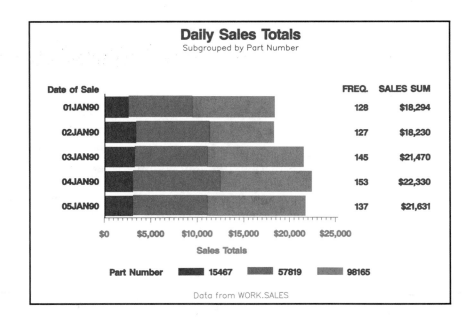

This example illustrates the following features:

□   The response axis is now the horizontal axis.

□   Totals for each bar are printed even though you removed the SUM option.

□   The bars are displayed from top to bottom; values are charted from left to right on the horizontal axis.

Creating and Enhancing Block Charts

To chart a block chart, first delete the AXIS statement and RAXIS= option (axes do not appear in block charts), then substitute the BLOCK statement for the HBAR statement.

Submit the following program statements to create a block chart:

```
title1 height=5 pct 'Daily Sales Totals';
title2 font=simplex 'Subgrouped by Part Number';
footnote color=red font=simplex 'Data from WORK.SALES';

pattern1 value=solid color=blue;
pattern2 value=solid color=green;
pattern3 value=solid color=red;
```

```
proc gchart data=sales;
   label date='Date of Sale'
         partnum='Part Number';
   format date date7. sales dollar7.;
   block date
         / discrete
           subgroup=partnum
           sumvar=sales
           patternid=subgroup;
run;
```

The results are shown in Output 3.15.

Output 3.15
Creating a Block
Chart

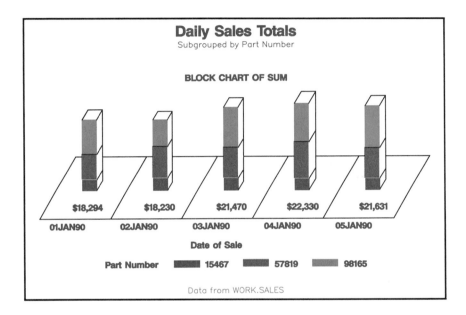

This example illustrates the following features:

□   The titles and footnote are where they were in the previous chart, but the chart now looks three-dimensional.

□   The default heading, BLOCK CHART OF SUM, can be deleted by using the NOHEADING option in the BLOCK statement.

□   The dollar amounts are printed underneath each block.

Chapter **4** Pie Charts

Introduction

In this chapter, you will learn to present statistical information in the form of a pie chart. Figure 4.1 shows a pie chart as well as a star chart, which you can also produce using the GCHART procedure.

Figure 4.1
Pie and Star Charts

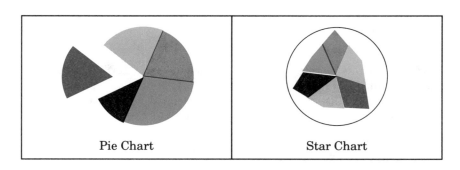

Pie Chart   Star Chart

When deciding which type of chart you want to use, consider that

□ pie charts show how part of your data relates to the rest of it and give a graphic representation of percentages of a whole through the slices of the pie. A slice is presented for each observation of the variable being charted. Labels and statistical values are displayed outside of the slices.

□ star charts show if an activity is in balance with its counterparts or is under control. The *spine* of each star slice (the line drawn in the middle of the slice) represents the middle value of the slice. The center of the star represents the lowest statistical value charted; the outside circle of the chart represents the highest value, and the radius of each spine represents the statistic for the variable (spine heights are similar in purpose to bar heights in a bar chart).

Whichever chart you choose, you use the same basic steps in the GCHART procedure with just a few variations for each chart.

Before beginning this chapter, make sure no global options are still in effect by submitting the following statement:

```
goptions reset=global;
```

Note: If you have not already done so in your current SAS session, enter the following GOPTIONS statement to make sure your output looks as much as possible like the examples in this book.

```
goptions gunit=pct
         cback=white
         htitle=6
         htext=3
         ftext=swissb
         ctext=blue;
```

Data for Sample Charts

In this chapter's examples you will use a SAS data set called SALES (GI01N03 in the sample library provided). This data set contains sales information for three parts sold by a fictitious company during the first work week of 1990. For the examples in this chapter, you will use only five of the SAS data set's ten variables:

BRANCH	is one of the two sales offices, either Atlanta or Boston.
PARTNUM	is a number assigned to the part.
DATE	is the date of sale.
AGENT	is the last name of the sales representative.
SALES	is the dollar amount of sales.

Note: If you did not create a SAS data set for these examples as shown in Chapter 1, "Producing Graphics Output in the SAS System," go back and do so now.

Understanding Chart Variables and GCHART Procedure Statistics

To learn about chart variables and the statistics used with the GCHART procedure, see Chapter 3, "Bar Charts." Note, however, that you will never use a pie chart to show cumulative frequency or cumulative percentage.

Creating Pie Charts

Many of the techniques you learned in Chapter 3 for creating vertical bar charts can also be used for pie charts. For example, to show the number of sales transactions according to the amount of sales, submit the following program statements:

```
proc gchart data=sales;
   format sales dollar4.;
   pie sales;
run;
```

The results are shown in Output 4.1.

Output 4.1
Creating a Simple
Pie Chart

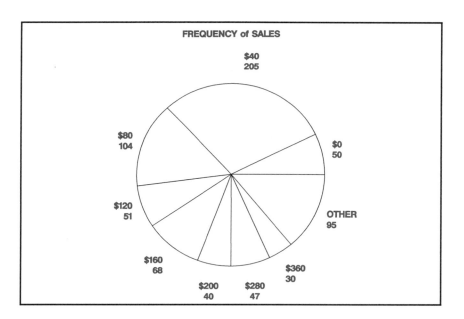

This example illustrates the following features:

□   A PROC statement specifies the GCHART procedure and the data set SALES. Each observation in the data set you are using corresponds to a sales transaction; Output 4.1 shows the frequency of observations.

□   The DOLLAR4. format makes the sales figures easier to read by displaying the numbers using 4 characters: a dollar sign and 3 digits.

□ The PIE statement specifies that a pie chart be created showing how often sales transactions occurred according to the amount of sale, which is recorded in the variable SALES.

□ The RUN statement begins the processing of statements.

□ A heading, FREQUENCY of SALES, is automatically placed at the top of the chart.

The pie chart is divided into slices, each a relative percentage of the whole pie. Remember that on numeric variable charts, each pie slice represents a range of numbers. For example, the largest slice of the pie shows you that 205 sales were for amounts between $20 and $60. This slice is labeled as $40, the dollar amount that falls in the middle of the range between $20 and $60. This middle value is known as the midpoint of the other values.

The dollar amounts the OTHER slice represents make up less than 4 percent of the total.

Choosing Variable Types

Like the vertical bar chart, the pie chart can use either character or numeric variables. The chart you just created used a numeric variable. To see how the pie chart deals with character variables and numeric variables whose values are charted individually, use examples similar to those used in Chapter 3 for the vertical bar chart.

To show the number of sales transactions for each day in the sample week, change the last SAS program you entered to chart the variable DATE, add the DISCRETE option to chart the values individually, then use the DATE7. format to make the SAS date values readable.

Submit the following program statements to chart the variable values individually:

```
proc gchart data=sales;
   format date date7.;
   pie date
       / discrete;
run;
```

The results are shown in Output 4.2.

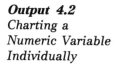

Output 4.2
Charting a
Numeric Variable
Individually

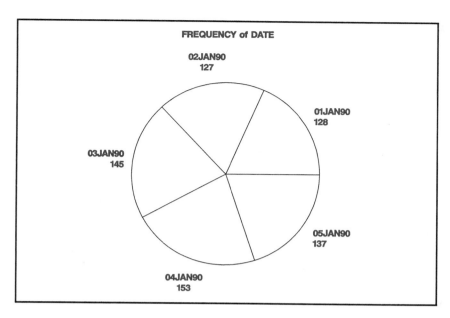

This example illustrates the following features:

□ The PIE statement now specifies that a chart be created showing how often sales transactions occurred according to the date of sale, which is recorded in the variable DATE.

□ The DISCRETE option specifies that each date be charted separately.

□ The DATE7. format puts the SAS date values into a readable form.

The chart shows that 128 sales were made on 01JAN90, 127 on 02JAN90, 145 on 03JAN90, and so on.
Note: Pie charts start their display of slices at the 3:00 position and rotate counterclockwise.

Charting a Character Variable

To chart the frequency of a character variable, change the chart variable to AGENT, then remove the DATE7. format and the DISCRETE option (character variables are automatically charted individually).
Submit the following program statements to chart the frequency of the variable AGENT:

```
proc gchart data=sales;
    pie agent;
run;
```

The results are shown in Output 4.3.

Output 4.3
Charting a
Character Variable

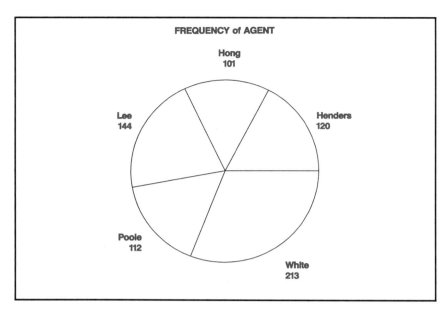

This example illustrates the following feature:

□ The PIE statement now specifies that a chart be created showing how often sales transactions occurred according to the sales agent, which is recorded in the variable AGENT.

The chart shows the specific number of sales transactions made by each agent. Output 4.3 shows that Henders had 120 sales, Hong had 101, and so on.

Specifying the Statistics Charted

Specifying statistics works the same with pie charts as it does with vertical bar charts. To show the number of sales transactions for each agent as a percentage of the total number of sales transactions, add the TYPE= option, assigning it the PERCENT statistic.

Submit the following program statements to chart the PERCENT statistic for the variable AGENT:

```
proc gchart data=sales;
   pie agent
        / type=percent;
run;
```

The results are shown in Output 4.4.

Output 4.4
Specifying a
Chart's Statistics

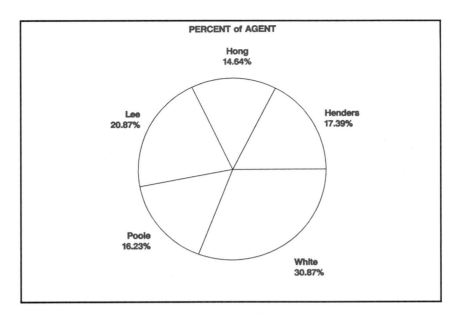

This example illustrates the following features:

□ The TYPE= option replaces the default FREQ statistic with the PERCENT statistic. The chart looks virtually the same as the previous one. Now, however, the number of sales transactions are expressed as relative percentages of the whole. For example, 17.39% of all sales transactions were made by Henders, 14.64% by Hong, and so on.

□ From a broader standpoint, this chart makes it easier to tell at a glance who had the highest number of sales and who had the fewest.

Charting Summary Variables

You can display the total or average values of a variable by using the SUMVAR= and TYPE= options. To show each agent's total amount of sales, change the statistic in the TYPE= option to SUM and specify SALES as the variable to be summarized using the SUMVAR= option. Also add the DOLLAR10.2 format to make the dollar amounts easier to read.

Submit the following program statements to display the average variable values:

```
proc gchart data=sales;
    format sales dollar10.2;
    pie agent
        / type=sum
            sumvar=sales;
run;
```

The results are shown in Output 4.5.

Output 4.5
Charting the Sum
of a Variable

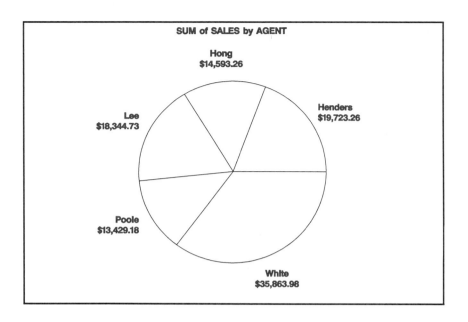

This example illustrates the following features:

□ The TYPE= option specifies the statistic, in this case SUM, to use on the variable specified in the SUMVAR= option. (SUM is the default statistic for the SUMVAR= option, so in this case it is not technically required. However, if you were trying to find the mean, you would have to enter TYPE=MEAN.)

□ The SUMVAR= option adds each day's values for the variable SALES, showing that during the first week in 1990, Henders had total sales of $19,723.26, Hong a total of $14,593.26, and so on. You can also compare the agents' relative percentages with each other by looking at the size of the slices.

□ The DOLLAR10.2 format adds dollar signs, commas, and two decimal places to the values for each slice.

Grouping Slices

You can organize a pie chart into groups based on a variable other than the one you are primarily charting by using the GROUP= option. Grouping produces a separate pie chart for each group.

To show the total amount of sales for the agents of each branch, add the GROUP= option, assigning it the variable BRANCH. Also, because the TYPE=SUM option is not technically needed, delete it from the program.

Submit the following program statements to group the pie slices:

```
proc gchart data=sales;
   format sales dollar10.2;
   pie agent
       / sumvar=sales
         group=branch;
run;
```

The results are shown in Output 4.6.

Output 4.6
Grouping Pie
Slices

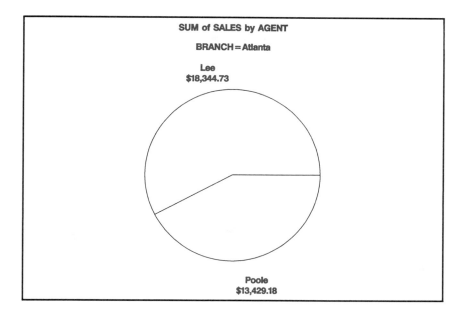

This example illustrates the following features:

□ The GROUP= option creates two separate pies, the first containing the slices for the the Atlanta branch, the second (not shown here) for the Boston branch.

□ Removing the TYPE= option does not affect the pie chart.

Enhancing a Pie Chart's Appearance

Now that you've learned how to create a pie chart, you need to learn how to add to and change its appearance. You have already learned how to use the FORMAT statement, but you can also

□ omit default headings

□ include titles, footnotes, and labels

□ change slice patterns and colors

□ offset and hide slices.

Omitting a Heading and Adding Titles and Footnotes

To omit the default heading of a pie chart, add the NOHEADING option. Delete the GROUP= option so the rest of the examples appear on one pie chart. Then, to label the chart, add TITLE and FOOTNOTE statements as you learned in the previous chapters.

Submit the following program statements to make these changes:

```
title color=red 'Sales '
      color=green 'for First Week of January, 1990';
footnote height=4 "&sysdate";

proc gchart data=sales;
   format sales dollar10.2;
   pie agent
       / sumvar=sales
         noheading;
run;
```

The results are shown in Output 4.7.

Output 4.7
Omitting a
Heading and
Adding a Title and
Footnote

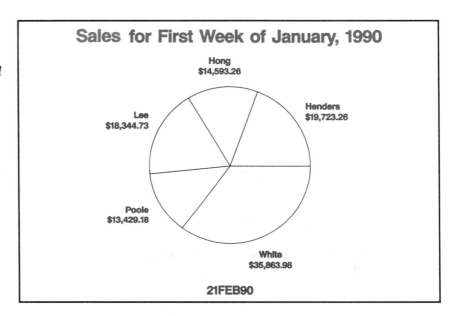

This example illustrates the following features:

□ The NOHEADING option removes the heading that appears by default at the top of pie, block, and star charts.

□ The title appears in the place of the heading. Notice that the word Sales is now red.

□ The footnote is centered below the pie chart by default. Notice the height of the footnote. Because you entered no unit of measurement for the height, the HEIGHT= option uses percent of display, the unit you specified in the GUNIT=PCT option of the GOPTIONS statement you entered earlier.

□ In the footnote, your entry of "&SYSDATE" causes the current date to be displayed.

Including Labels

Using the SLICE= and VALUE= options in the PIE statement, you can control the placement of the labels and statistics.

To connect the statistic (the value of SUMVAR=) with the slices, add the VALUE=ARROW option. To place the slice labels inside the slices, add the SLICE=INSIDE option.

Submit the following program statements to control the labels and statistics of your chart:

```
title color=red 'Sales '
      color=green 'for First Week of January, 1990';
footnote height=4 "&sysdate";

proc gchart data=sales;
   format sales dollar10.2;
   pie agent
       / sumvar=sales
         noheading
         value=arrow
         slice=inside;
run;
```

The results are shown in Output 4.8.

Output 4.8
Including Labels

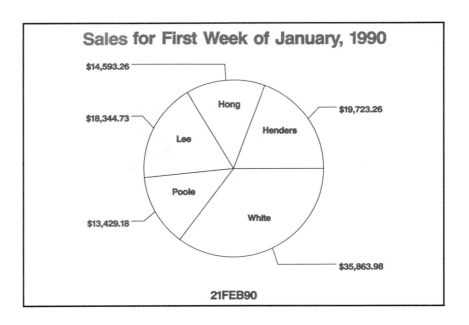

This example illustrates the following features:

□ The VALUE=ARROW option creates an arrow to connect the dollar amounts with their corresponding slices.

□ The SLICE=INSIDE option causes the agents' names to appear within the slices.

Adding Slice Patterns and Colors

You can add either a solid or crosshatched pattern to the pie slices using the FILL= option, which uses colors from the current colors list in rotation. For example, to fill the slices with solid colors, add the FILL=SOLID option. To make sure the labels show up inside all of the slices, add the CTEXT=RED option.

Submit the following program statements to create a solid pattern:

```
title color=red 'Sales '
      color=green 'for First Week of January, 1990';
footnote height=4 "&sysdate";

proc gchart data=sales;
   format sales dollar10.2;
   pie agent
      / sumvar=sales
        noheading
        value=arrow
        slice=inside
        fill=solid
        ctext=red;
run;
```

The results are shown in Output 4.9.

Output 4.9
Adding Patterns
and Colors

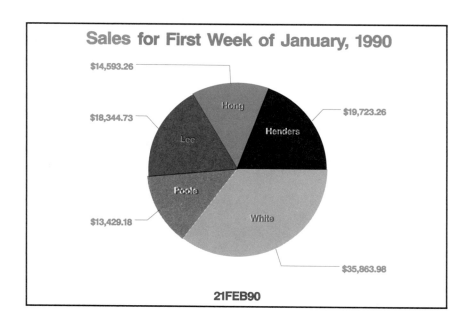

Sales for First Week of January, 1990

$14,593.26

$18,344.73

Hong

Henders

$19,723.26

Lee

Poole

White

$13,429.18

$35,863.98

21FEB90

This example illustrates the following features:

□ The FILL=SOLID option fills the slices with solid colors taken from your device's default colors list. The colors are selected in rotation; when all colors are used, the first one is used again, then the second, and so forth. You can also fill slices with crosshatching using the FILL=X option.

□ The CTEXT= option within the PIE statement changes only the color of the text relating to the pie (the labels and values), not the text for the titles or footnotes. Options affect only the statements they appear under.

Note: Your colors may be different than those shown in Output 4.9. If you have a red slice, its label will not show up because you specified the text color to be red in the CTEXT=RED option. If this is the case, choose a color that does not show up in any of the pie slices and use it instead of red in the CTEXT= option.

Offsetting Pie Slices

You may want to set a slice off from the rest of the pie to emphasize the data it illustrates. To *offset* a slice of the pie, add the EXPLODE= option for one specific value of a variable.

Submit the following program statements to offset the pie slice representing Lee:

```
title color=red 'Sales '
      color=green 'for First Week of January, 1990';
footnote height=4 "&sysdate";

proc gchart data=sales;
   format sales dollar10.2;
   pie agent
       / sumvar=sales
         noheading
         value=arrow
         slice=inside
         fill=solid
         ctext=red
         explode='Lee';
run;
```

The results are shown in Output 4.10.

Output 4.10
Exploding a Pie
Slice

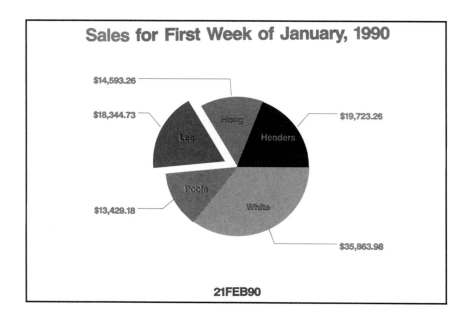

This example illustrates the following feature:

□   The EXPLODE= option offsets the slice for sales agent Lee from the rest of
the pie.

Note: The variable name must appear exactly as it does in the input data,
so if you entered LEE or lee, the slice would not be offset.

Making Pie Slices Invisible

Instead of offsetting a slice to emphasize it, you may want to make a slice
invisible to de-emphasize it. A good way to use the INVISIBLE= option in a
presentation is to show a pie with most of the slices invisible, then progressively
disclose those slices that are important. To make a slice invisible, remove the
EXPLODE= option and use the INVISIBLE= option.

Submit the following program statements to make the slice representing Lee
invisible:

```
title color=red 'Sales '
      color=green 'for First Week of January, 1990';
footnote height=4 "&sysdate";
```

```
proc gchart data=sales;
   format sales dollar10.2;
   pie agent
      / sumvar=sales
        noheading
        value=arrow
        slice=inside
        fill=solid
        ctext=red
        invisible='Lee';
run;
```

The results are shown in Output 4.11.

Output 4.11
Hiding a Pie Slice

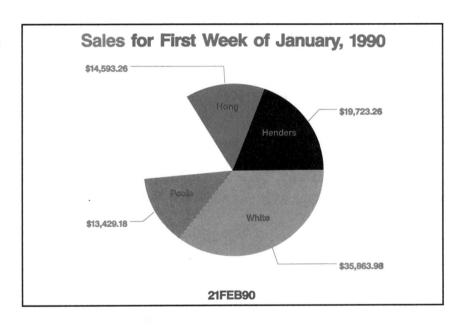

This example illustrates the following feature:

□   The INVISIBLE= option removes the slice for sales agent Lee.

Note: As with the EXPLODE= option, the variable name must appear exactly as it does in the input data, so if you entered LEE or lee, the slice would not be removed.

You now know how to create a simple pie chart. There are many more options and statements not covered in this book that you can use to customize and improve the appearance of your chart. See Chapter 8, "Gallery of Graphs," and *SAS/GRAPH Software: Reference, Version 6, First Edition, Volume 1* and *Volume 2* for more information.

Creating and Enhancing Star Charts

You can create and enhance star charts in much the same way as you just produced pie charts. For example, to create a star chart similar to the last pie chart you produced, substitute the STAR statement for the PIE statement. To enhance the star chart's appearance, delete the VALUE=, SLICE=, and INVISIBLE= options.

Submit the following program statements to create your star chart:

```
title color=red 'Sales '
      color=green 'for First Week of January, 1990';
footnote height=4 "&sysdate";

proc gchart data=sales;
   format sales dollar10.2;
    star agent
      / sumvar=sales
        noheading
        fill=solid;
run;
```

The results are shown in Output 4.12.

Output 4.12
Creating a Star
Chart

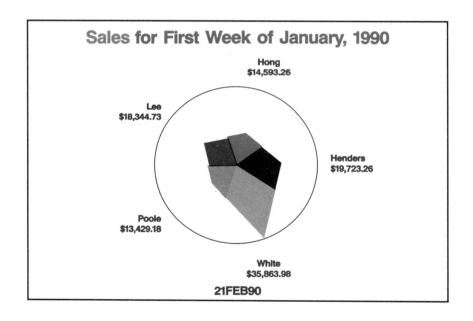

This example illustrates the following features:

□ The center of a star chart represents the lowest statistical value charted.

□ The middle of each variable value (the midpoint) on a star chart is depicted by the spine of each slice.

□ The outside circle of a star chart represents the highest value charted and touches the end of the spine of the highest statistical value.

Notice that the agents' sales amounts are out of balance, with a large difference between the lowest and highest dollar amounts of sale.

Chapter **5** Plots

Introduction

In this chapter, you will learn to display your data in the form of
two-dimensional plots. These plots are an effective way to show a trend in data
over a period of time, or to show the relationship of one variable to another.

Figure 5.1 shows three different plots that you can produce with the GPLOT
procedure: a line plot, a high-low plot, and a scatter plot. In each of these plots,
one variable is plotted on the horizontal axis, X, and a second variable is plotted
on the vertical axis, Y.

The plots you can produce using SAS/GRAPH software, which are depicted
in Figure 5.1, fall into one of three categories:

trends   show that every value of X has only one value of Y.

ranges   show that every value of X has multiple values of Y.

scattered data   show that every value of X can have one or more values of Y.

***Figure* 5.1**
Plotting Trends,
Ranges, and
Scattered Data

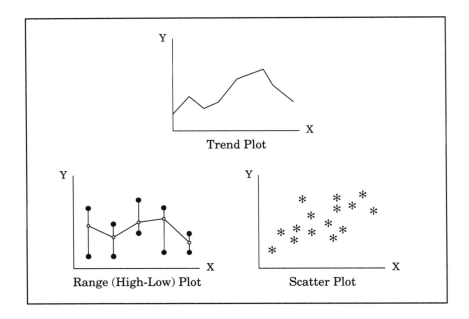

If your data fall into the first category, trends, you can use a straight line plot to show a trend or pattern in the data. For these plots, your data must be sorted in the proper sequence. For example, the data for a plot that shows sales versus date must be sorted by the date variable before it is plotted. This type of plot is discussed in "Plotting Trends or Patterns in Data" later in this chapter.

If the data you want to plot fall into one of the latter two categories, there is a wide range of plot types available to emphasize the unique relationships between your variables. These plots are useful as analytical tools, often answering questions such as "How does variable 1 affect the outcome of variable 2?" or "If I have this much of variable 1, what value should I expect for variable 2?" Examples of two of these plot types are discussed in "Plotting Data Dependency Relationships" later in this chapter. For a complete list of these plot types, see *SAS/GRAPH Software: Reference, Version 6, First Edition, Volume 2*.

The procedure for plotting data from any of the three categories is the same: you use a PLOT statement to request a plot of points, and you use a SYMBOL statement with options to control characteristics of the plot line and the plot symbols. The only differences between plotting trends, ranges, and scatter data are the values that you assign to the SYMBOL statement options.

Before beginning this chapter, make sure that no global options are still in effect by submitting the following statement:

```
goptions reset=global;
```

Note: If you have not already done so in your current SAS session, enter the following GOPTIONS statement to make sure your output looks as much as possible like the examples in this book.

```
goptions gunit=pct
         cback=white
         htitle=6
         htext=3
         ftext=swissb
         ctext=blue;
```

Data for Sample Plots

In this chapter's examples, you will use three SAS data sets from the file GI01N01 in the sample library provided. The three data sets are

DATE1   contains a summary of the Eastern Widgets Inc. first quarter sales transactions by week. You use this data set in the next section, "Plotting Trends or Patterns in Data," to plot the trends in sales and costs over the first quarter.

DATE2   contains a summary of the Eastern Widgets Inc. first quarter sales transactions by week for each part number. You use this data set to plot the trend in sales over the first quarter for each part number; each part number will be represented by a different plot line, and the plot lines will be defined in a legend at the bottom of the graph.

IRIS   contains the length and width measurements for a group of iris plant petals. You use this data set in "Plotting Data Dependency Relationships," later in this chapter, to create a scatter plot and a regression line that depict the relationship between petal length and petal width.

Note: If you did not create these SAS data sets as shown in Chapter 1, "Producing Graphics Output in the SAS System," go back and do so now. Now you are ready to proceed with the examples in this chapter.

Plotting Trends or Patterns in Data

You can use a plot in a variety of forms to portray a trend in data over time. In this section, you will use the data set DATE1 to produce a simple plot that shows a trend in sales figures for Eastern Widgets Inc. over the first quarter of 1990, and then you will see how to make some enhancements to this plot.

The data set DATE1 contains three variables:

DATE   represents an element of time (the date of the sale) and is plotted on the horizontal axis. In the data set, the values of DATE are listed in ascending order from the earliest date to the latest date. This is important when you are connecting the data points on your plot; the points are connected in the order that they appear in the data set. If your time variable values are not in the appropriate time sequence, you can use the SORT procedure to sort the data by the time variable before you plot the data points.

COST   represents the cost of filling sales orders, including replacing and repairing defective parts. Since COST is dependent on DATE, it is called a *dependent variable*. As a dependent variable, it is plotted on the vertical axis.

SALES   represents the dollar amount that customers paid for their purchases during a specific period of time, or on a specific date. Since SALES is dependent on DATE, it is a dependent variable. As a dependent variable, it is plotted on the vertical axis.

Producing a Simple Plot

To produce a plot of sales versus date using the data set DATE1, use a PLOT statement within the GPLOT procedure to identify the variables for the horizontal and vertical axes.

Submit the following program statements to produce a simple plot:

```
title1 color=green 'Sales Transactions';
footnote1 justify=right 'First Quarter, 1990  ';

proc gplot data=date1;
   format date date7. sales dollar8.;
   plot sales*date;
run;
```

The results are shown in Output 5.1

Output 5.1
Producing a
Simple Plot

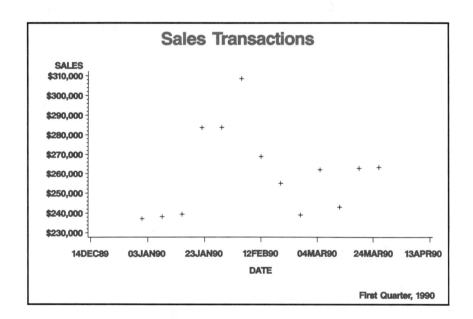

This example illustrates the following features:

□ The PROC GPLOT statement specifies the GPLOT procedure. The DATA= option identifies the SAS data set DATE1.

□ The PLOT statement specifies a plot of points. The first variable in the PLOT statement is plotted on the vertical axis; the second variable is plotted on the horizontal axis.

□ The FORMAT statement describes the way that the values of DATE and SALES are displayed on the plot.

□ The GPLOT procedure uses current values to scale and label the axes and to represent the data points.

Joining Plot Points

By default, the plot symbols in a plot are not connected. To emphasize the trend in the data from one data point to the next, you can connect the plot symbols.

The way in which you connect the points is called the *method of interpolation*; you control the method of interpolation by using the INTERPOL= option in the SYMBOL statement.

Submit the following program statements to join the data points with straight lines:

```
title1 color=green 'Sales Transactions';
footnote1 justify=right 'First Quarter, 1990  ';

symbol1 interpol=join;

proc gplot data=date1;
   format date date7. sales dollar8.;
   plot sales*date;
run;
```

The results are shown in Output 5.2.

Output 5.2
Connecting the
Plot Symbols

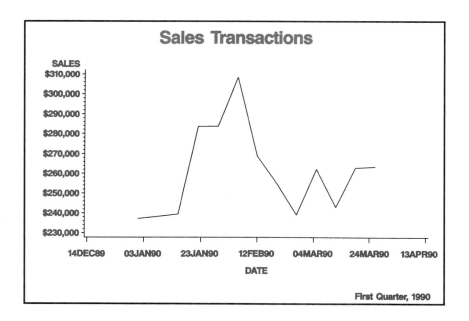

This example illustrates the following features:

□ The INTERPOL=JOIN option connects the points with straight lines.

□ The plot symbol that appeared in the previous plot has disappeared.

Changing the Plot Symbol

In addition to joining the plot symbols, you can also use SYMBOL statement options (such as the HEIGHT=, COLOR=, and VALUE= options) to control the size, shape, and color of the plot symbols.

Submit the following program statements to make the plotting symbol a large, red diamond:

```
title1 color=green 'Sales Transactions';
footnote1 justify=right 'First Quarter, 1990  ';

symbol1 interpol=join
        color=red
        value=diamond
        height=6;

proc gplot data=date1;
   format date date7. sales dollar8.;
   plot sales*date;
run;
```

The results are shown in Output 5.3.

Output 5.3
Changing the Plot
Symbols

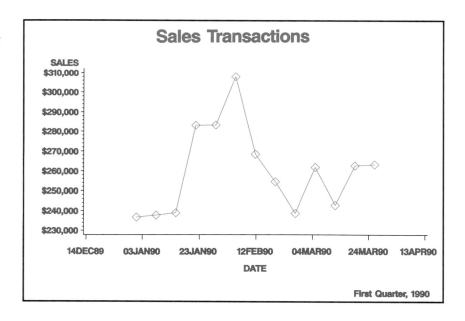

This example illustrates the following features:

□ The VALUE=DIAMOND option represents the data points with diamonds.

□ The COLOR=RED option makes the diamonds red.

□ The HEIGHT=6 option makes the height of the diamonds equal to 6 units. The unit of measurement is determined by the GUNIT= option you submitted earlier in the GOPTIONS statement. Thus, because you specified GUNIT=PCT, the height of the diamonds is 6 percent of the display area. The default unit of measurement is *character cells.* One character cell is the approximate area used to display one hardware character.

Modifying the Axes

As you have seen, the GPLOT procedure automatically scales and labels the coordinate axes. However, you can change the appearance, position, and content of the axes by using AXIS statements. The AXIS statements are assigned to the horizontal and vertical axes with the HAXIS= and the VAXIS= options in the PLOT statement. In this section, you will learn how to use AXIS statement options to label axes, order tick mark values, change tick mark values, and offset tick marks from the origin.

Labeling the Axes

So far, the GPLOT procedure has labeled each axis on your plots with the name of the variable represented by the axis. If the default labels are too vague or ambiguous, you can use the LABEL= option in an AXIS statement to define your own axis labels.

Submit the following program statements to customize the labels on your plot:

```
title1 color=green 'Sales Transactions';
footnote1 justify=right 'First Quarter, 1990  ';

symbol1 interpol=join
        color=red
        value=diamond
        height=6;

axis1 label=('Date of Sale');
axis2 label=('Total Sales');

proc gplot data=date1;
   format date date7. sales dollar8.;
   plot sales*date / haxis=axis1
                     vaxis=axis2;
run;
```

The results are shown in Output 5.4.

Output 5.4
Using AXIS
Statements to
Label and Offset
Axes

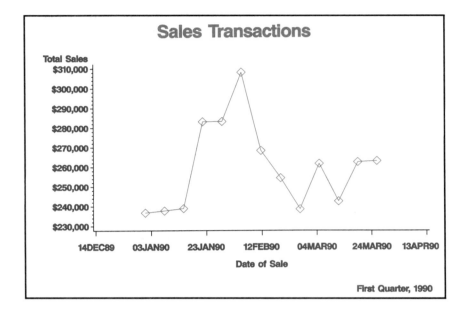

This example illustrates the following features:

□ The AXIS1 and AXIS2 statements create the AXIS definitions for the horizontal and vertical axes. The HAXIS=AXIS1 option in the PLOT statement assigns the AXIS1 definition to the horizontal axis. The VAXIS=AXIS2 option assigns the AXIS2 definition to the vertical axis.

□ The LABEL= option in the AXIS statement uses the text string that appears between the single quotes to label the axis.

Ordering Tick Mark Values

Unless you specify otherwise, the GPLOT procedure automatically selects the range of values to be plotted on each axis and then determines the order and placement of the tick marks.

You can control the range of values that are plotted on the axes and the interval between major tick marks by using the ORDER= option in the AXIS statement. In addition, you can offset the first major tick mark from the origin by using the OFFSET= option.

Submit the following program statements to customize the range of values on your plot:

```
title1 color=green 'Sales Transactions';
footnote1 justify=right 'First Quarter, 1990  ';

symbol1 interpol=join
        color=red
        value=diamond
        height=6;
```

```
axis1 label=('Date of Sale')
      offset=(2)
      order=('01JAN90'd to '26MAR90'd by 14);
axis2 label=('Total Sales')
      offset=(2)
      order=(230000 to 320000 by 30000);

proc gplot data=date1;
   format date date7. sales dollar8.;
   plot sales*date / haxis=axis1
                     vaxis=axis2;
run;
```

The results are shown in Output 5.5.

Output 5.5
Ordering Values
on the Axes

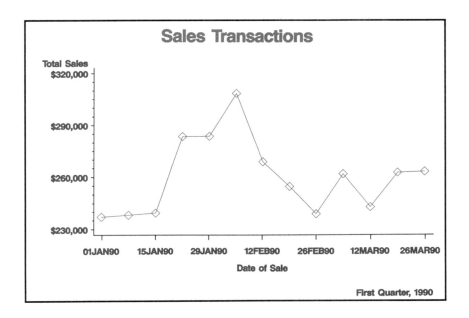

This example illustrates the following features:

□ The OFFSET= option places the first major tick mark 2 units from the origin and the last major tick mark 2 units from the end of the axis. (The unit of measurement is a percent of the display area, which you specified with the GUNITS=PCT option in the GOPTIONS statement you submitted earlier.)

□ The ORDER= option specifies the data values in the order that they are to appear on the axis. The values specified by the ORDER= option are the major tick mark values. These values are displayed at the major tick marks unless they are modified by the VALUE= option, as shown in the next example.

This plot emphasizes minor variations in week-to-week sales. If you wanted to illustrate the magnitude of weekly variations you could change the major tick mark values of the AXIS2 statement to ORDER=(0 to 350000 by 50000).

Note: In the ORDER= option for the AXIS1 statement, the SAS date value, 'DDMMMYY'd, creates a SAS date value from the date enclosed in the quotes. The GPLOT procedure increments the SAS date value by 14 days for each successive major tick mark.

Changing Tick Mark Values

In the preceding plots, the sales values would have been easier to read if the numbers were rounded to the nearest thousand. By using the VALUE= option in the AXIS2 statement, you can drop the last three zeros from the sales values. In addition to making this change, be sure to change the LABEL= option to indicate that the sales values on the vertical axis are now in thousands of dollars.

Submit the following program statements to change the sales values on your plot:

```
title1 color=green 'Sales Transactions';
footnote1 justify=right 'First Quarter, 1990  ';

symbol1 interpol=join
        color=red
        value=diamond
        height=6;

axis1 label=('Date of Sale')
      offset=(2)
      order=('01JAN90'd to '26MAR90'd by 14);
axis2 label=('Total Sales' justify=right '(thousands)')
      offset=(2)
      order=(230000 to 320000 by 30000)
      value=(t=1 '$230' t=2 '$260' t=3 '$290' t=4 '$320');

proc gplot data=date1;
   format date date7. sales dollar8.;
   plot sales*date / haxis=axis1
                     vaxis=axis2;
run;
```

The results are shown in Output 5.6.

Output 5.6
Changing Tick
Mark Values

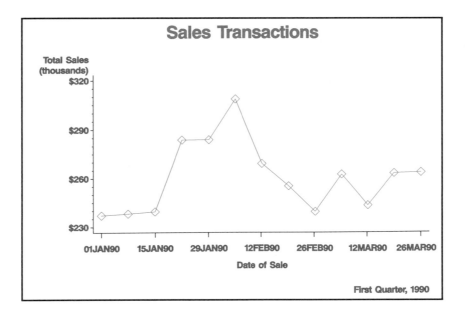

This example illustrates the following features:

□ The VALUE= option, using the T= parameter, assigns labels (enclosed in quotes) to each of the tick marks.

□ The LABEL= option in the AXIS2 statement has been changed to include (thousands). The JUSTIFY= parameter puts (thousands) on the line underneath Total Sales and right justifies it in relation to the vertical axis of the plot.

□ Because the labels you created in the AXIS2 statement replace the actual numbers that appeared in Output 5.5, the DOLLAR8. format for the variable SALES is not used.

Producing a Series of Plots

So far you have learned how to use the PLOT statement to generate one plot at a time. However, with the GPLOT procedure, you can use one PLOT statement to generate multiple plots. You can either produce a separate graph for each plot line or you can place all of the plot lines on the same graph.

For example, to compare the trend in sales with the trend in manufacturing costs for the same time period, you can change the TITLE statement to reflect the change in the plot, change the AXIS2 statement, add the COST value to the FORMAT statement, and add two new variables for the PLOT statement.

Submit the following program statements to make these changes:

```
title1 color=red
       font=triplex 'Total Costs and Sales';
footnote1 justify=right 'First Quarter, 1990  ';

symbol1 interpol=join
        color=red
        value=diamond
        height=6;

axis1 label=('Date of Sale')
      offset=(2)
      order=('01JAN90'd to '26MAR90'd by 14);
axis2 offset=(2);

proc gplot data=date1;
   format date date7. sales cost dollar8.;
   plot cost*date sales*date / haxis=axis1
                               vaxis=axis2;
run;
```

The results are shown in Output 5.7.

Output 5.7
*Producing a Series
of Plots*

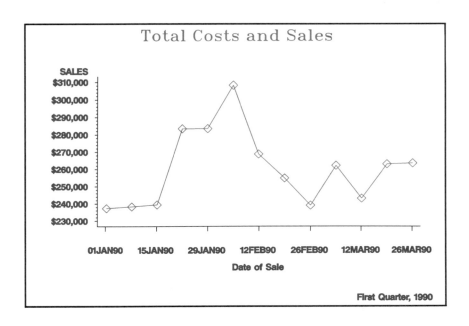

This example illustrates the following features:

□ The TITLE statement creates a new title in a different font and color.

□ The AXIS2 statement does not order and label the values as it did in the previous example.

□ The FORMAT statement now describes the way the values of COST are displayed.

□ The PLOT statement creates a new plot for the variables COST and DATE.

□ The vertical axis for each plot is scaled independently. You can force the vertical axes to use the same scale by adding the UNIFORM option in the PROC GPLOT statement.

Overlaying Multiple Plots

Instead of producing a separate graph for each plot, you can place both plots on the same set of axes by using the OVERLAY option in the PLOT statement. To give each line a different look on the overlay plot, use a different SYMBOL statement for each line. In addition, to help distinguish between the two plots, make some changes to the TITLE1 statement.

Submit the following program statements to create the overlay plot described above:

```
title1 color=red
       font=triplex 'Total Costs' color=green ' and Sales';
footnote1 justify=right 'First Quarter, 1990  ';

symbol1 interpol=join
        color=red
        value=none;

symbol2 interpol=join
        color=green
        value=none;

axis1 label=('Date of Sale')
      offset=(2)
      order=('01JAN90'd to '26MAR90'd by 14);
axis2 offset=(2)
      label=none;

proc gplot data=date1;
   format date date7. sales cost dollar8.;
   plot cost*date sales*date / haxis=axis1
                               vaxis=axis2
                               overlay;
run;
```

The results are shown in Output 5.8.

Output 5.8
Overlaying Plots

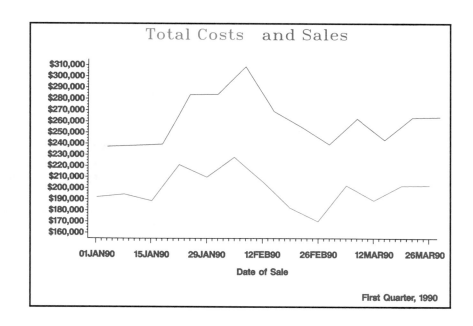

This example illustrates the following features:

□ The LABEL=NONE option in the AXIS2 statement removes the label for the vertical axis.

□ The SYMBOL2 statement creates a second SYMBOL definition to control the characteristics of the second plot line.

□ The title's color has changed, with the first part (Total Costs) appearing in red and the last part (and Sales) appearing in green.

Notice that now the vertical axis accommodates the entire range of dollar amounts for sales and manufacturing costs.

The plot overlay is useful for superimposing several plot lines on one set of coordinate axes; however, the OVERLAY option does not enable you to generate a corresponding legend at the bottom of the graph. If you want to generate a legend, see "Producing Plots with a Legend" later in this chapter.

Filling Areas with Colored Patterns

You can use PATTERN statements in conjunction with the AREAS= option to assign different color and pattern fills to different areas of your graph. By specifying colors and patterns in PATTERN statements, you can enhance the graph and direct attention to the relationship between the set of plotted values. In addition, add ORDER= and VALUE= options to the AXIS2 statement to specify the data values in the order that they are to appear and to label the major tick mark values.

▶ *Caution* . . . . *Be careful when you use this technique with the OVERLAY option.*
Because the GPLOT procedure fills areas from the horizontal axis up to the plot lines in the order that the plots are requested, always request the plots in order of increasing distance from the horizontal axis: request the lowest plot first. ▲

Submit the following program statements to fill in an area of your plot:

```
title1 color=red
       font=triplex 'Total Costs' color=green ' and Sales';
footnote1 justify=right 'First Quarter, 1990  ';

symbol1  interpol=join
         color=red
         value=none;
symbol2  interpol=join
         color=green
         value=none;

pattern1 color=red
         value=solid;
pattern2 color=green
         value=solid;

axis1 label=('Date of Sale')
      offset=(2)
      order=('01JAN90'd to '26MAR90'd by 14);
axis2 label=none
      offset=(2)
      order=(160000 to 320000 by 40000)
      value=(t=1 '$160' t=2 '$200' t=3 '$240' t=4 '$280' t=5 '$320');

proc gplot data=date1;
   format date date7. sales cost dollar8.;
   plot cost*date sales*date / haxis=axis1
                               vaxis=axis2
                               overlay
                               areas=2;
run;
```

The results are shown in Output 5.9.

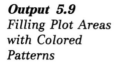

Output 5.9
*Filling Plot Areas
with Colored
Patterns*

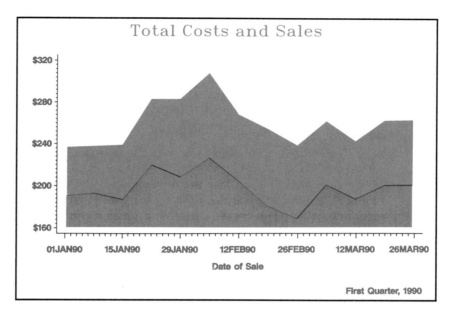

This example illustrates the following features:

□ The AREAS=2 option in the PLOT statement indicates that the areas under two curves should be filled. The GPLOT procedure fills the area between the horizontal axis and the first plot line first, the area between the first and second plot lines next, and so on. Because costs are lower than sales, the plot for cost versus date is requested first.

□ The VALUE=SOLID option in the PATTERN statement defines a solid fill pattern for the areas under the plots.

□ The COLOR= option in the PATTERN statement defines a red fill pattern for the first area and a green fill pattern for the second area.

□ The ORDER= and VALUE= options in the AXIS2 statement order and label the data values.

Producing Plots with a Legend

To produce a graph that contains a legend explaining each plot line, you must use a plotting technique known as *plotting by a third variable*. To plot by a third variable, your data set must contain a variable to be plotted on the horizontal axis and a variable to be plotted on the vertical axis, as well as a third variable whose values represent the individual plots that you want to produce. For example, to plot sales versus date for each of three different part numbers, you need the variables SALES and DATE, in addition to the variable PARTNUM, whose values are equal to the three part numbers.

In many cases, your data set may not contain a third variable. In this example, you will see how to restructure your data set in order to create the third variable.

Suppose that you want to work with the data in the data set DATE2 to plot sales versus date for each part number. The data set contains the following variables:

DATE is the date of sale.

PRT15467 is the dollar amount of the sales for part 15467.

PRT57819 is the dollar amount of the sales for part 57819.

PRT98165 is the dollar amount of the sales for part 98165.

Because the data set does not have one specific variable to represent the part numbers, you cannot use this data set to plot by part number. However, from this data set, you can create a new data set that can be used to plot by part number.

Submit the following program statements to create a new data set containing the variables SALES, DATE, and PARTNUM. (Text between /* and */ symbols is known as a SAS comment, used to document parts of a SAS program. Comments do not affect the program and do not have to be entered.)

```
   /* Create the data set BYPART from the data set DATE2 */
data bypart;
   set date2;

      /* Restructure the data so that there is one observation of */
      /* sales for each combination of date and part number       */
   drop prt15467 prt57819 prt98165;
   partnum=15467; sales=prt15467; output;
   partnum=57819; sales=prt57819; output;
   partnum=98165; sales=prt98165; output;
run;
```

To see the structure of the new data set, display the contents of BYPART by submitting the following program statements:

```
proc print data=bypart;
run;
```

The results are shown in Output 5.10.

Output 5.10
Displaying the
BYPART Data Set

```
                              The SAS System


                 OBS     DATE    PARTNUM     SALES

                  1     10958     15467      21591.93
                  2     10958     57819      94447.34
                  3     10958     98165     121135.61
                  4     10965     15467      22574.09
                  5     10965     57819      64554.91
                  6     10965     98165     151075.93
                  7     10972     15467      21878.07
                  8     10972     57819      74008.32
                  9     10972     98165     143517.23
                 10     10979     15467      20308.17
                 11     10979     57819      76783.63
                 12     10979     98165     186464.42
                 13     10986     15467      27747.80
                 14     10986     57819      97771.93
                 15     10986     98165     158143.81
                 16     10993     15467      26587.77
                 17     10993     57819     109364.64
                 18     10993     98165     172426.82
                 19     11000     15467      16642.49
                 20     11000     57819     105519.67
                 21     11000     98165     146658.51
                 22     11007     15467      24259.99
                 23     11007     57819      77737.65
```

In this data set, the variable values of PARTNUM represent the three part numbers: 15467, 57819, and 98165. When you request a plot by PARTNUM, you get three plot lines, one for each of the three part numbers.

To create such a plot, make the following changes to your last SAS program: add a third SYMBOL statement, remove the PATTERN statements, change the AXIS2 statement, change the name of the data set in the GPLOT procedure, remove the COST value from the FORMAT statement, change the PLOT statement, and change the TITLE1 statement to reflect the change in the plot.

Submit the following program statements to create a plot with three plot lines:

```
title1 color=red
       font=triplex
       height=7 pct 'Sales Transactions';
footnote1 justify=right 'First Quarter, 1990  ';

symbol1  interpol=join
         color=red
         value=none;
symbol2  interpol=join
         color=green
         value=none;
symbol3  interpol=join
         color=blue
         value=none;

axis1 label=('Date of Sale')
      offset=(2)
      order=('01JAN90'd to '26MAR90'd by 14);
axis2 label= ('Total Sales')
      offset=(2);
```

```
proc gplot data=bypart;
   format date date7. sales dollar8.;
   plot sales*date=partnum / haxis=axis1
                             vaxis=axis2;
run;
```

The results are shown in Output 5.11.

Output 5.11
Generating a
Legend

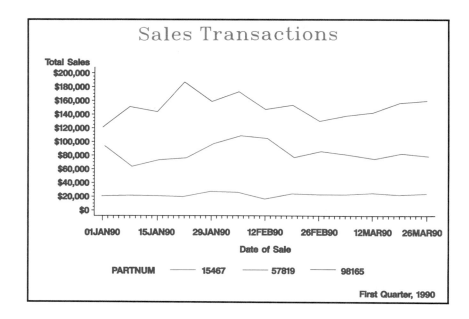

This example illustrates the following features:

☐ The plot request SALES*DATE=PARTNUM draws one plot on the graph for each value of PARTNUM and produces a legend defining the values of PARTNUM.

☐ The legend uses the variable name PARTNUM for the legend label and the variable values for the legend value descriptions.

☐ The SYMBOL statements are assigned to the values of PARTNUM in ascending order. For example, the value 15467 is assigned to SYMBOL1.

☐ The SYMBOL statement also assigns each plot line a different color.

☐ The TITLE1 statement defines a new title.

Plotting Data Dependency Relationships

So far, you have concentrated on plots that show a trend or pattern in the data over time. However, if your variables represent elements other than time, you can use plots such as scatter plots or regression lines to explore other types of relationships between variables.

Generating a Scatter Plot

The scatter plot uses data points to show the relationship between two variables. The scatter plot is similar to the default plot you produced showing the sales trend for Eastern Widgets Inc. during the first quarter of 1990. The only difference between these plots is the organization of the data: in the trend plot, each value of X (DATE) had only one value of Y (SALES). In the scatter plot, each value of X can have one or more values of Y.

Because the scatter plot is used to emphasize individual data points, the data points are not connected.

Submit the following program statements to investigate the relationship between the length and width of the petals from a sample of iris plants:

```
title1 color=red
       font=triplex 'Study of Iris Petals';
title2 color=red
       font=duplex
       height=5 pct 'Petal Length vs. Petal Width';
footnote1 color=red justify=left '  Sample Size=36';

symbol1 color=green
        value=star
        height=6
        interpol=none;

axis1 color=blue
      offset=(2)
      label=('Length');
axis2 color=blue
      offset=(2)
      label=('Width');

proc gplot data=iris;
   plot petalwid*petallen / haxis=axis1
                            vaxis=axis2;
run;
```

The results are shown in Output 5.12.

Output 5.12
Producing a
Scatter Plot

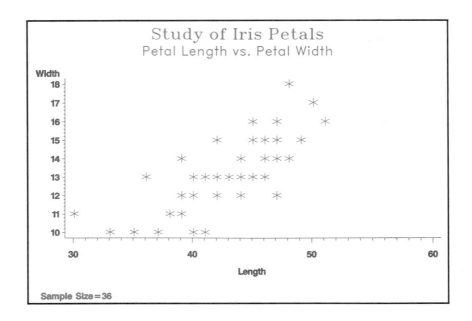

This example illustrates the following features:

□ The COLOR=, VALUE=, and HEIGHT= options in the SYMBOL1 statement specify that the symbols be green stars with a height of 6 percent of the display area.

□ The INTERPOL=NONE option in the SYMBOL1 statement specifies that the symbols should not be connected.

This scatter plot illustrates that there is definitely a positive correlation between the petal length and petal width; as the petal gets longer, it also gets wider.

Showing Regression Analysis

The scatter plot you just produced explores the strength of the relationship between petal length and petal width. Based on this relationship, you can predict, or estimate, the petal width if you know the petal length. This is called *regression analysis*.

In using regression analysis, you can request that PROC GPLOT fit a line through the data points using the INTERPOL= option in the SYMBOL statement.

Submit the following program statements to draw a regression line and confidence limits:

```
title1 color=red
       font=triplex 'Study of Iris Petals';
title2 color=red
       font=duplex
       height=5 pct 'Petal Length vs. Petal Width';
footnote1 color=red justify=left '  Sample Size=36';

symbol1 color=green
        value=star
        height=6
        interpol=rlclm95;

axis1 color=blue
      offset=(2)
      label=('Length');
axis2 color=blue
      offset=(2)
      label=('Width');

proc gplot data=iris;
   plot petalwid*petallen / haxis=axis1
                            vaxis=axis2;
run;
```

The results are shown in Output 5.13.

Output 5.13
Drawing a Regression Line and Confidence Limits

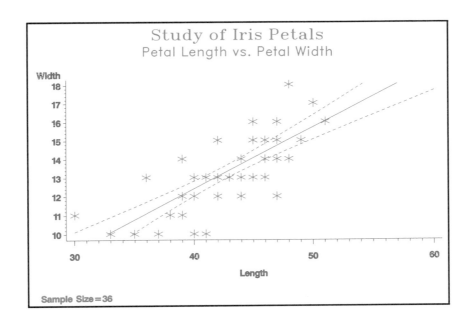

This example illustrates the following features:

□ The RL value in the INTERPOL= option requests that PROC GPLOT fit a linear (straight) regression line through the data points.

□ The CLM value of 95 in the INTERPOL= option draws the 95 percent confidence limits for a mean predicted value. For example, you can predict, with 95 percent certainty, that a group of iris petals with a length of 40 centimeters will have an average width in the interval between 12 and 13 centimeters.

Chapter **6** Maps

Introduction

For many applications, the best way to represent your data is in the form of a map: a visual representation of a geographic area. You can use the GMAP procedure to produce four types of maps. This chapter shows you how to produce the most common type: choropleth maps. These maps use color and pattern combinations to show variations in variable values with respect to map areas.

By displaying data in the form of a map, you can

☐ summarize data that vary according to geographic area

☐ highlight regional differences

☐ show trends and variations of data between geographic areas.

To produce a map with the GMAP procedure you need two SAS data sets: a map data set and a response data set. The map data set contains a set of coordinates that represent the boundaries of the map areas; this is the data set that you use to draw the map outlines. The response data set contains the data that you want to evaluate and display on the map.

Before beginning this chapter, make sure that no global options are still in effect by submitting the following statement:

```
goptions reset=global;
```

Note: If you have not already done so in your current SAS session, enter the following GOPTIONS statement to make sure your output looks as much as possible like the examples in this book.

```
goptions gunit=pct
         cback=white
         htitle=6
         htext=3
         ftext=swissb
         ctext=blue;
```

Setting Up Map and Response Data Sets

The maps in this chapter are produced using the response data set STSALE. If you did not create this data set as shown in Chapter 1, "Producing Graphics Output in the SAS System," go back and do so now.

To produce your maps, you can use a collection of map data sets that are provided with SAS/GRAPH software. These maps include, but are not limited to

US   contains coordinates for state boundaries of the 50 United States and for Washington, D.C.

COUNTIES   contains coordinates for county boundaries in the 48 continental United States, as well as Hawaii and Puerto Rico.

CANADA   contains coordinates for boundaries of Canadian provinces and census districts.

Other common geographic areas available include countries of the world and standard metropolitan statistical areas (SMSA).

The map data sets that are provided with SAS/GRAPH software should be located in a SAS data library at your site. To determine the name of this SAS data library, consult your SAS Software Consultant.

Once you have located the map data sets, use the following program statement to assign the libref MAPS to the SAS data library:

```
libname maps 'SAS-data-library';
```

Be sure to replace *SAS-data-library* with the appropriate library name for your site. If your site externally assigns a libref of MAPS, you do not need to issue the LIBNAME statement.

Now you are ready to use the response data set STSALE with the examples in this chapter.

Selecting Map Data Sets

If you are producing a map of a geographic area, chances are that there is at least one map data set that will meet your needs. To select the map data set that best represents the geographic areas with which you want to work, you can

□ browse a list of the available map data sets

□ list detailed information about specific map data sets.

Browsing Map Data Sets

By using a PROC DATASETS statement, you can produce a list of the available map data sets:

```
proc datasets lib=maps;
run;
```

Browse through the list of map data sets until you find the data set US. This is the map data set that you will use in this chapter to display sales and cost figures for the Boston and Atlanta branches of Eastern Widgets Inc.

Note: The map data set US is *projected*; it contains coordinate values that are well suited for plotting on a flat surface or two-dimensional plane. However, some of the map data sets provided with SAS/GRAPH software are not already projected. For unprojected maps, which appear backwards, each point on the map is stored as a spherical coordinate (radians latitude and radians longitude). Projection translates the data so that the map can be drawn on a flat plane (your graph) with a minimum of distortion. For more information about projecting map data sets, see *SAS/GRAPH Software: Reference, Version 6, First Edition, Volume 2.*

Finding Detailed Information

Before you use the map data set US to produce a map, use the CONTENTS procedure to see what type of variables are used in the data set.

Submit the following program statements to view the data set variables:

```
proc contents data=maps.US;
run;
```

The results are shown in Output 6.1.

Output 6.1
Variables in a
Data Set

```
                              The SAS System

                           CONTENTS PROCEDURE

   Data Set Name: MAPS.US                    Observations:          1526
   Member Type:   DATA                       Variables:             4
   Engine:        V606                       Indexes:               0
   Created:       06NOV89:14:12:23           Observation Length:    14
   Last Modified: 06NOV89:14:12:23           Deleted Observations:  0
   Data Set Type:                            Compressed:            NO
   Label:

        -----Alphabetic List of Variables and Attributes-----

    #     Variable   Type   Len   Pos    Label
   -------------------------------------------------------------
    2     SEGMENT    Num     3     3     State Segment Number
    1     STATE      Num     3     0     State FIPS Code
    3     X          Num     4     6     X Coordinate
    4     Y          Num     4    10     Y Coordinate

            -----Engine/Host Dependent Information-----

    Data Set Page Size:         6144
    Number of Data Set Pages:   7
    First Data Page:            1
    Max Obs per Page:           235
```

This example shows that the data set US contains

□ a numeric variable named SEGMENT, used for states with separate areas (such as the multiple boundaries of Michigan).

□ a numeric variable named STATE that uniquely identifies the map areas, the areas for which boundaries are drawn, as states. This variable is called the *ID variable*. The label associated with the ID variable STATE, State FIPS Code, is an acronym for the Federal Information Processing Standard Code. The label indicates that the variable values of STATE are the two-digit state FIPS codes (for example, the FIPS code for North Carolina is 37).

□ a numeric variable named X that contains the horizontal coordinate of each boundary point.

□ a numeric variable named Y that contains the vertical coordinate of each boundary point.

For more information about map data sets, see SAS Technical Report P-196, *SAS/GRAPH Software: Map Data Sets, Release 6.06.*

Using Response Data Sets

Like map data sets, response data sets contain at least one ID variable to indicate the unit areas of the map. In addition, response data sets contain one or more response variables. The response variables contain the data you want to evaluate and display.

For example, suppose that you want to evaluate several categories of data:

□ total sales within the company by state

□ total cost of production by state

□ sales and costs within the company by branch

□ region covered by each sales branch.

You can find this data in the response data set STSALE. Submit the following program statements to see the contents of the data set:

```
proc print data=stsale;
run;
```

The results are shown in Output 6.2.

Output 6.2
Printing the
Contents of a Data
Set

```
                              The SAS System


        OBS    BRANCH    STATENM    STATE       COST        SALES

          1    Atlanta     AL          1     $100,114     $143,033
          2    Atlanta     FL         12     $128,847     $165,439
          3    Atlanta     GA         13     $124,973     $170,580
          4    Atlanta     MS         28     $125,888     $158,545
          5    Atlanta     NC         37     $138,401     $184,858
          6    Atlanta     SC         45     $135,598     $164,653
          7    Atlanta     TN         47     $141,735     $182,314
          8    Boston      CT          9     $118,441     $145,174
          9    Boston      DE         10     $141,572     $172,517
         10    Boston      ME         23     $115,734     $146,375
         11    Boston      MD         24     $135,245     $191,364
         12    Boston      MA         25     $133,870     $179,174
         13    Boston      NH         33     $122,705     $168,358
         14    Boston      NJ         34     $112,805     $157,887
         15    Boston      NY         36     $138,362     $186,441
         16    Boston      PA         42     $127,158     $165,347
         17    Boston      RI         44     $133,875     $173,783
         18    Boston      VT         50     $146,092     $177,036
         19    Boston      VA         51     $135,252     $195,959
         20    Boston      WV         54     $126,076     $155,766
```

This example illustrates the following variables of this response data set:

□ three unit identification (ID) variables:

STATENM	uses the postal abbreviation to identify states.
STATE	uses the two-digit FIPS code to identify states.
BRANCH	identifies the sales branches (Boston or Atlanta).

□ two response variables:

SALES	represents the total sales by state.
COST	represents the total cost (to the company) of producing the parts, including replacing and repairing defective parts.

Linking Map and Response Data Sets

In order to use your response data set, STSALE, with the map data set, US, the two data sets must have at least one common ID variable (the same name, length, and type). In this example, the variable STATE is in both data sets. In both the map and response data sets, STATE contains the two-digit, numeric FIPS codes. Therefore, the GMAP procedure can use STATE to link the two data sets and produce the maps.

Using the FIPS Code

If your response data set had not included the variable STATE containing the FIPS codes, you could have used functions in base SAS software to convert the two-letter state postal abbreviations in STATENM to their corresponding FIPS codes.

Submit the following program statements for one way to add FIPS codes to the response data set if they are not already there:

```
data stsale;
   set stsale;
   state=stfips(statenm);
run;
```

For more information on FIPS codes, see *SAS Language: Reference, Version 6, First Edition.*

Producing Choropleth Maps

A choropleth map displays data using colors and patterns in the map areas to represent the magnitude of a response variable. For example, you may want to produce a map showing the level of sales for each state in the Boston and Atlanta branches.

Submit the following program statements to produce such a map:

```
title1 color=red 'Total Sales by State';
title2 'First Quarter, 1990';
footnote1 color=green justify=left '  Choropleth Map';

proc gmap map=maps.us data=stsale;
   id state;
   choro sales;
run;
```

The results are shown in Output 6.3.

Output 6.3
Producing a
Choropleth Map

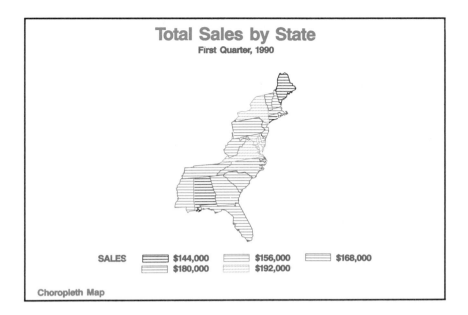

This example illustrates the following features:

□ The PROC GMAP statement runs the GMAP procedure. The MAP= option identifies the map data set and the DATA= option identifies the response data set.

□ The ID statement indicates that the variable STATE identifies the unit areas on the map.

□ The CHORO statement uses the response variable SALES to request a choropleth map showing the sales for each state.

□ The sales figures in the legend are displayed using a DOLLAR10. format. The format is stored as part of the DATA step in the data set STSALE. Because the format is stored as a part of the DATA step in the data set STSALE, it is not necessary to specify the format in the PROC step.

Including Areas with No Response Values

By default, the GMAP procedure draws only the map areas that are needed to display the data. To include those states that do not display data, add the ALL option to the PROC GMAP statement. To control the color of the state outlines and the legend text, use the the CEMPTY=, COUTLINE=, and CTEXT= options in the CHORO statement. To make the map areas where the data are represented appear in solid colors, add a PATTERN statement.

Submit the following program statements to include the remaining states:

```
title1 color=red 'Total Sales by State';
title2 'First Quarter, 1990';
footnote1 color=green justify=left ' Choropleth Map';

pattern value=solid;

proc gmap all map=maps.us data=stsale;
   id state;
   choro sales / cempty=green
                         coutline=red
                         ctext=green;
run;
```

The results are shown in Output 6.4.

Output 6.4
Displaying All
Map Areas

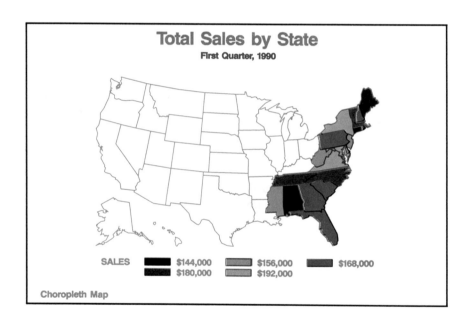

This example illustrates the following features:

□ The ALL option in the PROC GMAP statement requests that all map areas be drawn regardless of whether they display data.

□ The CEMPTY= option defines a green outline color for those map areas that do not display data.

□ The COUTLINE= option defines a red outline color for those map areas that do display data.

□ The CTEXT= option defines a green text color for the legend.

□ The PATTERN statement changes the shading pattern from lines to solid colors. The colors are chosen from your device's colors list; if the procedure needs more colors, it goes back through the colors list.

Working with Numeric Values

As you have seen, when the response variable is numeric, the GMAP procedure assumes that variable values are continuous and automatically groups the values into ranges, or response levels. Each response level has a numeric value equal to the median of its range of values.

You can control the ranges that are used to set the response levels by using the following options in the CHORO statement:

LEVELS=   sets a number of response levels.

MIDPOINTS=   defines the response levels explicitly.

DISCRETE   requests a response level for each unique value.

Defining the Number of Response Levels

When the response variable is continuous, you can specify the number of different response levels to be graphed by adding the LEVELS= option in the CHORO statement. In addition, remove the ALL option from the PROC GMAP statement and the CEMPTY= option from the CHORO statement to focus on the areas displaying data.

Submit the following program statements to set the response level:

```
title1 color=red 'Total Sales by State';
title2 'First Quarter, 1990';
footnote1 color=green justify=left ' Choropleth Map';

pattern value=solid;

proc gmap map=maps.us data=stsale;
   id state;
   choro sales / coutline=red
                 ctext=green
                 levels=3 ;
run;
```

The results are shown in Output 6.5.

Output 6.5
Changing the
Number of
Response Levels

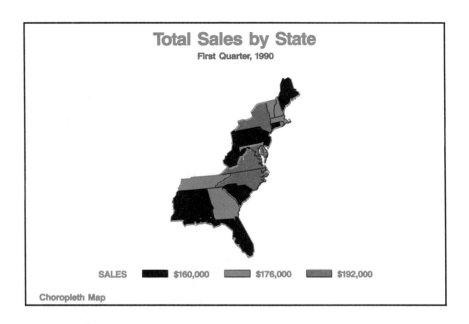

This example illustrates the following features:

□ As the legend indicates, the number of response levels has been decreased from five to three in the LEVELS= option. SAS/GRAPH software selects the response levels.

□ By removing the ALL option, you reduced the map's area to the states containing data to be displayed.

Defining Response Levels Explicitly

If you want to assign specific values to the response levels, you can use the MIDPOINTS = option instead of the LEVELS= option.

Submit the following program statements to assign these values:

```
title1 color=red 'Total Sales by State';
title2 'First Quarter, 1990';
footnote1 color=green justify=left '  Choropleth Map';

pattern value=solid;

proc gmap map=maps.us data=stsale;
   id state;
   choro sales / coutline=red
                 ctext=green
                 midpoints=150000 to 195000 by 15000;
run;
```

The results are shown in Output 6.6.

Output 6.6
Defining Response
Levels Explicitly

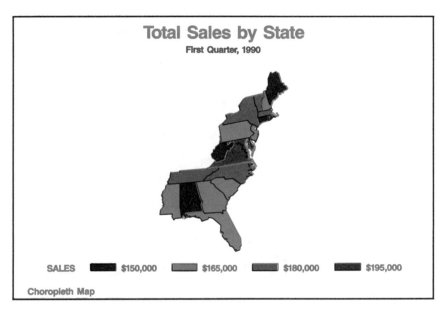

This example illustrates the following feature:

□ The legend reflects the midpoints you specified in the MIDPOINTS= option. In the previous example, SAS/GRAPH software compared them for you.

Using Discrete Numeric Values

To have a different response level for each unique value of SALES, use the DISCRETE option instead of the MIDPOINTS= option. In addition, limit the map to the Atlanta branch's area by using the WHERE= option in the GMAP procedure.

Submit the following program statements to create different response levels for each value:

```
title1 color=red 'Total Sales by State';
title2 'First Quarter, 1990';
footnote1 color=green justify=left '  Choropleth Map';

pattern value=solid;

proc gmap map=maps.us
           data=stsale (where=(branch='Atlanta'));
   id state;
   choro sales / coutline=red
                 ctext=green
                 discrete;
run;
```

The results are shown in Output 6.7.

Output 6.7
Using Discrete
Numeric Values

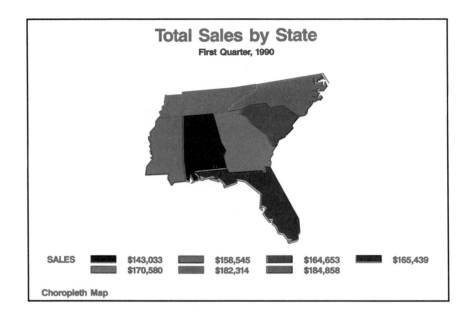

This example illustrates the following features:

□ The DISCRETE option shows separate values of the SALES variable instead of finding the midpoints as shown in Output 6.6.

□ The WHERE= option limits the map to states associated with the Atlanta branch.

Working with Character Values

If you want to produce a map showing the regions that each sales branch covers, you need to change some information in your program statements. Change the response variable SALES in the CHORO statement to BRANCH in order to use its values as response levels. Because you want to display both sales branches, be sure to remove the WHERE= option from the PROC GMAP statement. Also, because the values of the BRANCH variable are character instead of numeric and therefore are automatically mapped separately, remove the DISCRETE option from the CHORO statement. Finally, change the title to match the change in the map.

Submit the following program statements to produce these changes:

```
title1 color=red 'States Assigned to Sales Branches';
title2 'First Quarter, 1990';
footnote1 color=green justify=left '  Choropleth Map';

pattern value=solid;

proc gmap map=maps.us data=stsale;
   id state;
   choro branch / coutline=red
                  ctext=green;
run;
```

The results are shown in Output 6.8.

Output 6.8
Assigning
Character
Midpoints

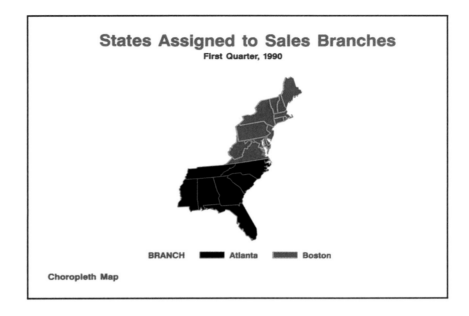

This example illustrates the following features:

□ The CHORO statement uses the response variable BRANCH to request a choropleth map showing the states assigned to each sales branch.

□ In using the BRANCH variable, the CHORO statement automatically maps each value of the variable as a separate category. The same effect could have been achieved by specifying MIDPOINTS='BOSTON' 'ATLANTA' as an option in the CHORO statement.

□ The new title assigned by the TITLE1 statement reflects the change in the purpose of the map.

Controlling Patterns and Colors

You can control colors and patterns for each response level by using PATTERN statements to create pattern definitions. Change the PATTERN statement already included and add another one.

Submit the following program statements to change the colors of your map:

```
title1 color=red 'States Assigned to Sales Branches';
title2 'First Quarter, 1990';
footnote1 color=green justify=left '  Choropleth Map';

pattern1 value=solid  color=blue;
pattern2 value=solid  color=green;

proc gmap map=maps.us data=stsale;
   id state;
   choro branch / coutline=red
                  ctext=green;
run;
```

The results are shown in Output 6.9.

Output 6.9
Adding Colors and Patterns

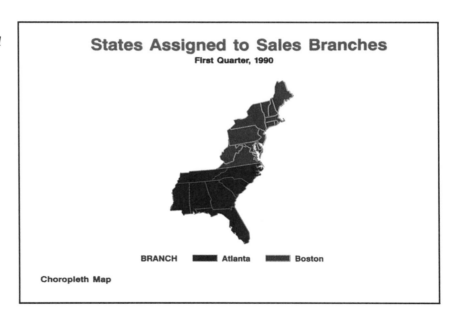

This example illustrates the following features:

☐ The VALUE= option in the PATTERN statement defines the fill pattern associated with the pattern definition. You can also specify slanted lines or empty fill values.

☐ The COLOR= option in the PATTERN statement specifies the color of the fill pattern.

Chapter **7** Text Slides

Introduction

As shown earlier in Chapter 2, "Titles and Footnotes," you can generate simple text slides by using the TITLE and FOOTNOTE statements with the GSLIDE procedure. In this chapter, you will learn to use the NOTE statement, which can also be used with the GSLIDE procedure.

In addition, you will learn to

□ use special characters to highlight text

□ position text

□ draw lines.

Before beginning this chapter, make sure that no global options are still in effect by submitting the following statement:

```
goptions reset=global;
```

Note: If you did not complete Chapter 1, "Producing Graphics Output in the SAS System," enter the following GOPTIONS statement to make sure your output looks as much as possible like the examples in this book.

```
goptions gunit=pct
         cback=white
         htitle=6
         htext=3
         ftext=swissb
         ctext=blue;
```

Displaying Text

To create a text slide that presents the total first quarter sales of each sales branch (Atlanta and Boston) in Eastern Widgets Inc., submit the following program statements:

```
title1 height=11 pct 'Total Sales by Branch';
title3 height=7 pct  'First Quarter, 1990';
footnote1 height=5 pct justify=right font=swissi
          color=red    'Eastern Widgets Inc.:'
          color=green '  $3,373,000';

proc gslide;
   note height=9 pct 'Atlanta    $1,169,000';
   note height=9 pct 'Boston     $2,204,000';
run;
```

The results are shown in Output 7.1.

Output 7.1
Displaying Text

Total Sales by Branch

First Quarter, 1990

Atlanta $1,169,000
Boston $2,204,000

Eastern Widgets Inc.: $3,373,000

This example illustrates the following features:

□ The PROC GSLIDE statement runs the GSLIDE procedure to create text slides.

□ The TITLE statements define the text for the two titles at the top of the slide. The FOOTNOTE statement defines the text for the footnote at the bottom of the slide. The area between the titles and the footnotes is called the *procedure output area*. This is the area in which the notes are displayed.

□ The NOTE statements define the text that is displayed in the procedure output area. Each new NOTE statement starts a new line of text, and the text is displayed in the order that the notes are specified in your program.

By default, the notes are left-justified and start at the top of the procedure output area.

□ NOTE statements are local, not global; therefore, notes must be defined inside the GSLIDE procedure. NOTE statements stay in effect until you quit the procedure or end your SAS session.

□ The NOTE statement uses the same options as the TITLE and FOOTNOTE statements. The options precede the text strings they modify, and they remain in effect until they are respecified within the statement or until the statement ends.

  □ The FONT=SWISSI option in the FOOTNOTE1 statement assigns the Swiss Italic type style to the footnote. Because the NOTE statements do not use a FONT= option in this example, the GSLIDE procedure uses the default type style (Swiss Bold, specified earlier in the FTEXT= option) for the notes, as it also does for the titles.

  □ The COLOR= option in the FOOTNOTE statement makes the character portion of the footnote red and the numeric dollar amount in the footnote green.

  □ The HEIGHT= option specifies the size of the characters in the TITLE, NOTE, and FOOTNOTE statements.

Using Special Characters

You can enhance your text slide by using special characters or symbols with the text. For example, to display a bullet in front of each item in your list, add the FONT= option.

Submit the following program statements to add bullets in front of the notes Atlanta and Boston:

```
title1 height=11 pct 'Total Sales by Branch';
title3 height=7 pct 'First Quarter, 1990';
footnote1 height=5 pct
          justify=right
          font=swissi
          color=red 'Eastern Widgets Inc.:'
          color=green '  $3,373,000';

proc gslide;
   note height=9 pct
        font=special '  J'
        font=swiss '  Atlanta       $1,169,000' ;
   note height=9 pct
        font=special '  J'
        font=swiss '  Boston        $2,204,000' ;
run;
```

The results are shown in Output 7.2.

Output 7.2
Creating a
Bulleted List

Total Sales by Branch

First Quarter, 1990

- Atlanta $1,169,000
- Boston $2,204,000

Eastern Widgets Inc.: $3,373,000

This example illustrates the following features:

□ The FONT=SPECIAL option displays the symbol associated with the letter J from the special character font. The FONT=SWISS option changes the type style to Swiss before printing any text.

□ The space between the initial quotation mark and the first letter of a note shows up on the slide (such as the space between the bullet and Atlanta).

Moving Text

By default, the notes are left-justified on the text slide in the order that they are entered in your SAS program. However, you can place the notes explicitly anywhere in the procedure output area by using the MOVE= option.

Submit the following program statements to move the notes to a new location in the procedure output area:

```
title1 height=11 pct 'Total Sales by Branch';
title3 height=7 pct 'First Quarter, 1990';
footnote1 height=5 pct
         justify=right
         font=swissi
         color=red 'Eastern Widgets Inc.:'
         color=green '  $3,373,000';
```

```
proc gslide;
   note move=(15 pct,45 pct)
            color=red
            height=9 pct
            font=special ' J'
            font=swiss ' Atlanta'
         move=(50 pct,45 pct)
            color=green
            '$1,169,000'
         move=(15 pct,30 pct)
            color=red
            height=9 pct
            font=special ' J'
            font=swiss ' Boston'
         move=(50 pct,30 pct)
            color=green
            '$2,204,000';
   run;
```

The results are shown in Output 7.3.

Output 7.3
Controlling the
Text Position

Total Sales by Branch

First Quarter, 1990

- Atlanta $1,169,000
- Boston $2,204,000

Eastern Widgets Inc.: $3,373,000

This example illustrates the following features:

□ The MOVE= option in the NOTE statement moves the text to the specified coordinates. Notice there is now only one NOTE statement. The coordinates are specified from the lower-left corner of the display, aligning the text and the dollar signs. The coordinate units can be in inches, centimeters, cells, or display percentage.

□ The COLOR= option in the NOTE statements makes the branch names red and the dollar amounts green.

Drawing Lines

In addition to placing text and special characters on your text slide, you can also draw lines on the slide to enhance your presentation. For example, you may want to draw one line above the list of sales branches and one below the list.

Submit the following program statements to draw these two lines:

```
title1 height=11 pct 'Total Sales by Branch';
title3 height=7 pct 'First Quarter, 1990';
footnote1 height=5 pct
          justify=right
          font=swissi
          color=red 'Eastern Widgets Inc.:'
          color=green '  $3,373,000';

proc gslide;
   note draw=(5 pct,60 pct,95 pct,60 pct);
   note move=(15 pct,45 pct)
             color=red
             height=9 pct
             font=special ' J'
             font=swiss ' Atlanta'
          move=(50 pct,45 pct)
             color=green
             '$1,169,000'
          move=(15 pct,30 pct)
             color=red
             height=9 pct
             font=special ' J'
             font=swiss ' Boston'
          move=(50 pct,30 pct)
             color=green
             '$2,204,000';
   note draw=(5 pct,15 pct,95 pct,15 pct);
run;
```

The results are shown in Output 7.4.

Output 7.4
Adding Lines to
Text Slides

Total Sales by Branch

First Quarter, 1990

- Atlanta $1,169,000
- Boston $2,204,000

Eastern Widgets Inc.: $3,373,000

This example illustrates the following feature:

□ The DRAW= option draws a line connecting the endpoints represented by the absolute coordinate pairs: (x1,y1,x2,y2).

□ The top line is drawn *from* the point at (5 pct,60 pct) *to* the point at (95 pct,60 pct).

□ The bottom line is drawn *from* the point at (5 pct,15 pct) *to* the point at (95 pct,15 pct).

Chapter **8** Gallery of Graphs

Introduction

In this book you learned how to create

- □ text slides
- □ bar charts
- □ block charts
- □ pie charts
- □ star charts
- □ plots
- □ maps.

However, you have only scratched the surface of the functions and features SAS/GRAPH software and other related SAS software offer you.

The gallery of graphs presented in this chapter shows you some of these features and functions of SAS/GRAPH software and related SAS software not covered elsewhere in this book. A brief description accompanies each graph.

Templates in the GREPLAY procedure combine the figures from the GMAP and GCHART procedures to produce Figure 8.1. The Annotate facility places labels on the AGE axis and the mileage and human figures (which are symbols in the MARKER font) in the bars.

Figure 8.1
Overlaying a Map with a Bar Chart

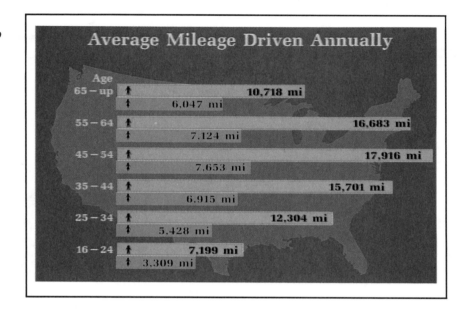

Templates in the GREPLAY procedure combine the figures from the GMAP and GCHART procedures to produce Figure 8.2. The Annotate facility places the numbers in the bars.

Figure 8.2
Combining and Labeling Graphs

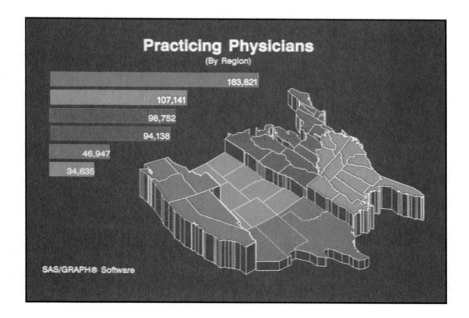

Templates in the GREPLAY procedure combine the figures from the GCHART procedure to produce Figure 8.3. The GSLIDE procedure produces the title.

Figure 8.3
Using the GSLIDE
Procedure on
Combined Graphs

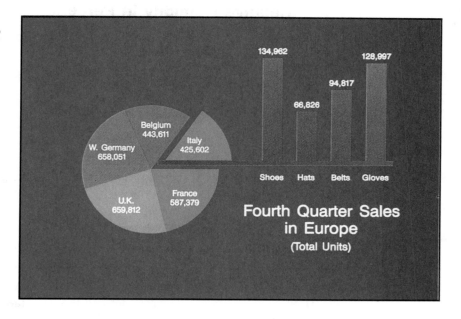

The GPLOT procedure creates a plot and the LEGEND statement displays a legend inside the plot to produce Figure 8.4.

Figure 8.4
Placing a Legend
Inside a Plot

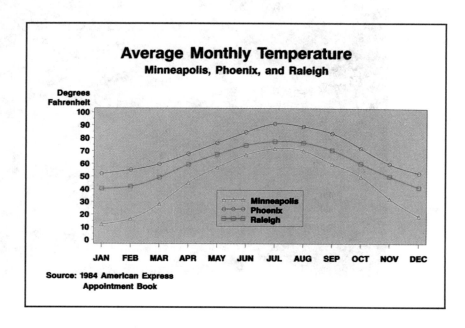

The G3D procedure creates a three-dimensional plot to produce Figure 8.5.

Figure 8.5
Creating a
Three-Dimensional
Plot

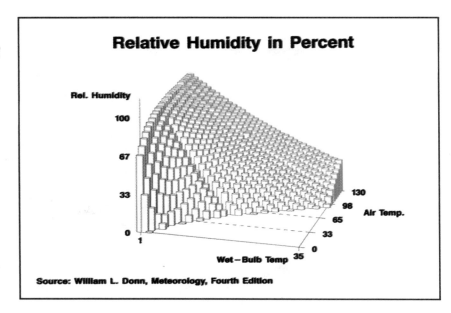

The G3D procedure creates a surface plot and the Annotate facility creates labels to produce Figure 8.6.

Figure 8.6
Creating and
Labeling a
Three-Dimensional
Plot

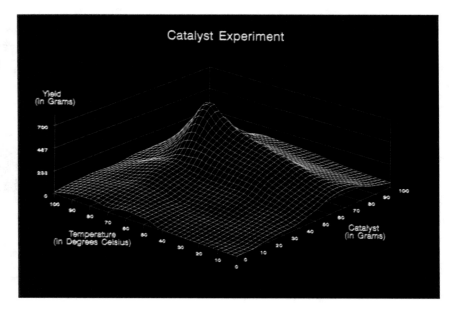

Templates in the GREPLAY procedure combine the figures from the GMAP and GCHART procedures to produce Figure 8.7. The Annotate facility provides the lines and labels.

Figure 8.7
Displaying and Labeling Multiple Graphs

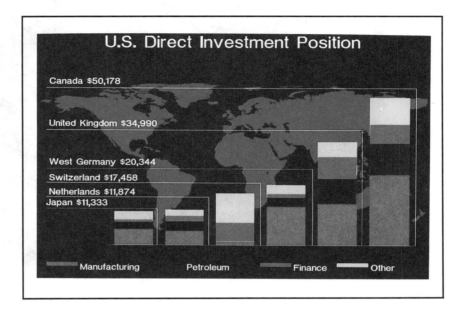

Templates in the GREPLAY procedure combine the figures from the GMAP and GPLOT procedures to produce Figure 8.8. The Annotate facility places red dots at site locations.

Figure 8.8
Overlaying a Map with a Plot

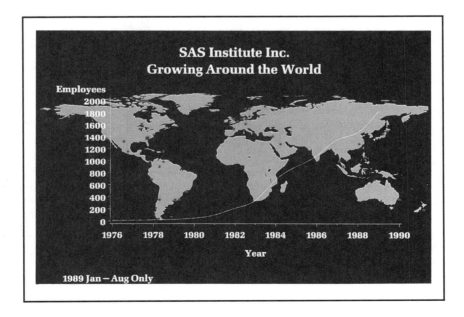

SAS/QC software creates a control chart to produce Figure 8.9.

Figure 8.9
*Creating a Graph
Using SAS/QC
Software*

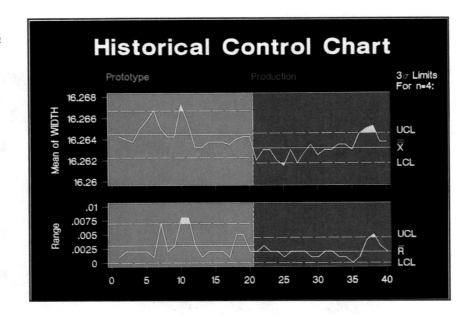

The Annotate facility creates a population tree to produce Figure 8.10.

Figure 8.10
*Creating a
Population Tree
Using the
Annotate Facility*

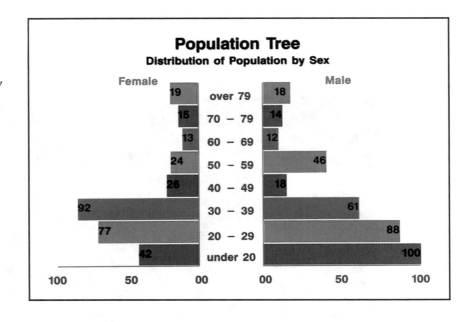

Glossary

absolute coordinates
coordinates measured from the origin (0,0) of the coordinate system. See also the entry for relative coordinates.

axis
the scale on which the values of the *x*, *y*, or *z* coordinate are represented. In SAS/GRAPH documentation, the term *axis* may also refer collectively to the axis line, the major and minor tick marks, the major tick mark values, and the axis label.

cell
a unit of measure defined by the number of rows and the number of columns in the graphics output area.

chart statistic
the statistical value calculated for the chart variable: frequency, cumulative frequency, percentage, cumulative percentage, sum, mean, or any combination of these values.

chart variable
a variable in the input data set used to categorize the data represented on the chart.

colors list
the list of foreground colors available for the graphics output. The colors list is either the default list established from the device entry or the list specified by the COLORS= graphics option and the COLOR= options in other statements. The colors specified in COLOR= options in any statement must be valid for the device.

convert
to change a SAS file from its original format to a format appropriate to another version of the SAS System under the same operating system. Use the V5TOV6 procedure to convert SAS/GRAPH files from Version 5 to Release 6.06.

coordinates
values representing the position of a data point or a graphics element. A point on a graph has a unique location specified by its coordinates: (*x*, *y*, *z*). Each coordinate represents a distance along an axis, which is measured from the origin of the coordinate system.

dependent variable
1) a variable whose value depends on the value of another variable or variables. 2) a variable that is a function of one or more independent variables. In a two-dimensional plot, the dependent variable is plotted on the *y* (vertical) axis. In a three-dimensional plot, the dependent variable is plotted on the *z* axis.

device driver
a set of routines that generate specific commands needed to display a graph on a particular device.

device parameter

a value in a device entry that defines a default behavior of a device driver. Some device parameters can be overridden by graphics options. See also the entry for graphics option.

display

the area of the monitor that displays what the software presents to you.

fill pattern

the pattern (lines, cross-hatching, and so on) or solid color used to fill an area in a graph. A fill pattern with no color or pattern is an empty pattern.

font

a complete set of all the characters of the same design and style. In SAS/GRAPH software, size is specified separately. The characters in a font can be figures or symbols as well as alphanumeric characters. See also the entry for type style.

graph

1) a visual representation of data showing the variation of a variable in comparison to one or more other variables. 2) graphics output.

graphics device

any terminal, printer, or other output device capable of displaying or producing a hardcopy of graphics output.

graphics option

a value specified in a GOPTIONS statement that controls some attribute of the graphics output. The values specified remain in effect only for the duration of the SAS session. Some graphics options override device parameters.

graphics output

output from a graphics program. It can be stored, displayed, or printed. Device-dependent output can be sent directly to a device. Device-independent output must be processed by a device driver before being sent to a graphics device.

group variable

a variable in the input data set used to categorize chart variable values into groups that are separately represented on the graph.

independent variable

a variable that does not depend on the value of another variable; in a two-dimensional plot, the independent variable is usually plotted on the x (horizontal) axis.

justify

to position text in relation to the left or right margin or the center of the line.

label

1) the text that names the variable associated with an axis, a legend, or a bubble in a bubble plot. By default, this text is the name of a variable or of a label previously assigned with a LABEL statement. The text of a label also can be specified with the LABEL= option. 2) in pie and star charts, the midpoint value and the value of the chart statistic for a slice or spine.

legend

a visual key to graphic elements in a graph.

major tick mark

a primary element on the scale of an axis. In SAS/GRAPH software, major tick mark locations are chosen automatically but can be specified explicitly. See also the entry for minor tick mark.

map

a graphic representation of an area, often a geographic area, but also any other area of any size.

midpoint

a value that identifies categories of chart variable data represented on a graph. A midpoint value represents a range of values or a single value.

minor tick mark

a tick mark between major tick marks. Minor tick marks do not display values. The number of minor tick marks displayed is determined either by default by the procedure or explicitly with options. See also the entry for major tick mark.

offset

1) on an axis, the distance from the axis origin to the first major tick mark or to the middle of the first bar, or the distance from the last major tick mark or from the middle of the last bar to the end of the axis line. 2) in a legend, the distance between the edge of the legend or legend frame and the axis frame or the border surrounding the graphics output area.

origin

1) in a coordinate system, the location of (0,0). 2) the intersection of coordinate axes.

pattern type

the set of fill patterns that are valid for a particular type of graph. The PATTERN statement supports three pattern types: bar and block patterns, map and plot patterns, and pie and star patterns. See also the entry for fill pattern.

regression analysis

an analysis of the relationship between two variables, expressed as a mathematical function. On a scatter plot, this relationship is diagrammed as a line drawn through data points, either a straight line (simple regression) or a curve (higher-order regression).

relative coordinates

coordinates measured from a point other than the origin, usually from the endpoint of the last object drawn. See also the entry for absolute coordinates.

response variable

in the GMAP procedure, a SAS data set variable containing a value to be represented in conjunction with a map unit area (for example by filling the area with a particular pattern or by drawing a block of representative height in the area).

SAS catalog

a SAS file that is a member of a SAS data library and that stores many different kinds of information in smaller units called catalog entries. SAS/GRAPH software uses device, template, font, color map, key map, and device map entries, as well as entries that contain graphics output.

SAS data library

a collection of one or more SAS files that are recognized by the SAS System. Each file is a member of the library.

spine

a line in a star chart used to represent the relative value of the chart statistic for a midpoint. Spines are drawn outward from the center of the chart.

subgroup variable

the variable in the input data set for a chart that is used to create segments of the bars on the chart.

type style

a typeface design and its variations, for example, Swiss, Swiss Bold, and Swiss Italic. See also the entry for font.

unit area

a polygon or group of polygons on a map, for example, a state, province, or country. In a map data set, a unit area consists of all the observations with the same values for the unit area identification variables. (The ID statement specifies which variable or variables in the map data set are unit area identification variables.)

value

1) on an axis, the text that labels a major tick mark. 2) in a legend, the lines, bars, and shapes that the legend explains. 3) the value of a variable.

window

a sizable, movable object on the display in which a user interacts with a program.

Index

our Turn

n you spare five minutes? We want to know what you think about
S/GRAPH Software: Introduction, Version 6, First Edition. Because we are
nstantly revising the documentation, we would like your comments on
w to improve it. Please respond to the questions below by filling in the
nks or checking (✔) the boxes (as many as are needed to answer each
estion). We also welcome comments on additional pages; just fold them
side of this postage-paid form and mail them to
S Institute.

ho Are You?

Which of the categories below best describe your industry?

☐ academic   ☐ insurance
☐ communications   ☐ manufacturing
☐ computers (hardware/software) ☐ pharmaceutical
☐ finance/banking   ☐ utilities
☐ government   ☐ other: _____
☐ health care

Which of the categories below best describe your job?

☐ computer programmer   ☐ supervisor/manager
☐ computer user, but not a   ☐ student
   programmer
☐ other: _____

How long have you been using SAS/GRAPH software?

☐ fewer than six months   ☐ one to three years
☐ six months to one year   ☐ three or more years

What is your level of expertise with SAS/GRAPH software?
(circle the number that applies)

Beginner   Intermediate User   Expert
1   2   3   4   5

List the SAS software you have used other than SAS/GRAPH software
(for example, base SAS, SAS/AF, SAS/FSP, and so on). If you have not
used any other SAS software, write "None." _____

How long have you used other SAS software products (not including
SAS/GRAPH software)?

☐ no previous use   ☐ one to three years
☐ fewer than six months   ☐ three or more years
☐ six months to one year

How long have you used software *other* than SAS software?

☐ no previous use   ☐ one to three years
☐ fewer than six months   ☐ three or more years
☐ six months to one year

hat Kind of Computer System Do You Have?

Under what operating system(s) are you running SAS/GRAPH
software?

_____

Which method(s) do you use to run SAS/GRAPH software?

☐ batch mode   ☐ interactive line mode
☐ SAS Display Manager System ☐ noninteractive line mode

What kind of graphics output device(s) do you have available?

☐ graphics terminal   ☐ printer
☐ plotter   ☐ camera
☐ none   ☐ other(s): _____

w and When Did You Use This Book?

Approximately what percentage of your work time is spent using
SAS/GRAPH software?

☐ 1–10%   ☐ 26–50%   ☐ 76–100%
☐ 11–25%   ☐ 51–75%

2. Approximately how long did it take you to complete this book?
_____ hours.

3. Number the chapters in the order you read them, leaving blank any you
did not read.

☐ Using This Book   ☐ 5, "Plots"
☐ 1, "Producing Graphics Output ☐ 6, "Maps"
   in the SAS System"   ☐ 7, "Text Slides"
☐ 2, "Titles and Footnotes"   ☐ 8, "Gallery of Graphs"
☐ 3, "Bar Charts"
☐ 4, "Pie Charts"

4. Did you work through this book in one sitting?
☐ Yes   ☐ No

5. If you did not work through this book in one sitting, how easy or difficult
was it to start again from where you left off?

Easy   Difficult
1   2   3   4   5

6. How did you acquire this copy of *SAS/GRAPH Software: Introduction*?

☐ you bought it personally   ☐ this is your company's only copy
☐ your company owns it, but this ☐ you borrowed it
   is your personal copy   ☐ other: _____
☐ your company owns it, and you
   share it with several people

How Easy Is This Book to Use?

1. List the chapters that were especially useful to you:

_____ _____ _____

_____ _____ _____

2. List the chapters that gave you too little information:

_____ _____ _____

_____ _____ _____

3. List functions and features that should have been explained in this book
and were not:

_____

_____

4. Did you find this book too basic or too technical?

Too   Too
Basic   Just Right   Technical
1   2   3   4   5

5. List topics that you found confusing:

_____

_____

6. a. Did you find the examples in this book helpful?

☐ they helped you use SAS/GRAPH software in your job
☐ they were not relevant to your use of SAS/GRAPH software

b. If they were not relevant, what types of examples do you need?

_____

_____

7. List any chapters that need more examples:

_____ _____ _____

_____ _____ _____

8. Other comments:

_____

_____

How Easy Is SAS/GRAPH Software to Use?

1. List the areas of SAS/GRAPH software that you had particular difficulty in using or understanding:

_____ _____ _____

_____ _____ _____

2. How often did this book help you solve these difficulties?

☐ always   ☐ rarely
☐ often   ☐ never
☐ occasionally   ☐ did not consult the book

Thank you for your time and effort. If you or your company would like a copy of the *Publications Catalog*, which lists available documentation from SAS Institute, please enter the following information:

Name _____ Date _____

Organization _____

Telephone _____

Address _____ _____

City _____ State _____ ZIP Code _____

FOLD THIS PORTION BACK FIRST

BUSINESS REPLY MAIL

FIRST CLASS   PERMIT NO. 64   CARY, NC

POSTAGE WILL BE PAID BY ADDRESSEE

SAS Institute Inc.
SAS Campus Drive
Cary, NC 27513